Testimonials

I started the third year not knowing what I wanted to do. After a semester of Dr Collins' PAD course, I knew what I wanted to do, how I was going to achieve it, and what I would do if it didn't happen. Although it was a lot of hard work, I got my foot in the door of a highly competitive industry and now have a career in market research. I can honestly say that I owe my first job to Dr Collins' course.

Jacqueline Stead, a graduate of UEA

Benjamin's enthusiastic advice at my university media fair ensured that I presented my future employers with a CV and covering letter that was as focused, and as relevant, to their needs as possible. I got the first job that I applied for, and I've just completed my first six months as an account executive in a successful full-service marketing communications agency. I'm really enjoying it.

Sandra Doran, a graduate of UEA

Dr Collins' PAD course proved invaluable in training and preparing me for various teaching interviews.

Phil Sheppard, a graduate of UEA

Before being on Dr Collins' course I never looked forward; since then I've never looked back. I learnt some essential tips and techniques which helped me get an interview for every job I have applied for ... I think that putting it all together into one book available to everyone is a brilliant idea. It should be essential reading to anyone who wants to pursue a successful career.

Rachel Spencer, ACA, a graduate of UEA

As an undergraduate, Dr Collins' course gave me the opportunity to develop and recognise my own skills and abilities and how to promote and apply them to the job market. I learnt how to best present the choices which I have made since graduating, in particular my decision to travel and work abroad. Three years after graduating I continue to refer to the PAD course material and am now pleased to see an updated version of this available in book form.

Sharon Wetherall, a graduate of UEA

I was able to see a copy of this book in draft form at a time when I was looking to move from post-university jobs into a career. I found the book to be very thorough and made the process a whole lot less daunting. It gave me tips and advice to swell my confidence for the all-important interviews.

Lisa Baldwin, a graduate of Brunel University

The only drawback to completing this unit is the constant pressure from friends, who did not take the unit, to help them with their CVs and applications.

Vanessa Williams, a current UEA student

It is becoming ever more important for graduates to present themselves in a professional manner to prospective employers.

Sarah Wilesmith, HR Director for an international bank, USA

In today's dynamic job market, graduates have to think about their marketability well in advance of leaving university. Dr Collins' course provides the competitive edge they need to start as successfully as they mean to go on.

Abigail Kirk-Walker, a UEA graduate

Turn Your Degree Into a Career

To James,

Good luck,

Benjamin Scott.

13.08.09.

Turn your
DEGREE
into a
CAREER

A STEP-BY-STEP GUIDE TO ACHIEVING YOUR DREAM CAREER

Dr Michael Collins & Benjamin Scott

howtobooks

First published in 2003 by
How To Books Ltd, 3 Newtec Place,
Magdalen Road, Oxford OX4 1RE. United Kingdom.
Tel: (01865) 793806. Fax: (01865) 248780.
email: info@howtobooks.co.uk
http://www.howtobooks.co.uk

British Library Cataloguing in Publication Data
A catalogue record for this book is available from the British
Library

Cover design by Baseline Arts Ltd, Oxford
Produced for How To Books by Deer Park Productions
Typeset by PDQ Typesetting, Newcastle-under-Lyme, Staffs.
Printed and bound in Great Britain by Cromwell Press,
Trowbridge, Wiltshire
Authors' photograph by Jacqueline Wyatt

NOTE: The material contained in this book is set out in good
faith for general guidance and no liability can be accepted
for loss or expense incurred as a result of relying in particular
circumstances on statements made in the book. The laws and
regulations are complex and liable to change, and readers should
check the current position with the relevant authorities before
making personal arrangements.

Contents

About the Authors

This book uses the experience of teaching a successful course in job-hunting, run at the University of East Anglia, as well as the experiences and feedback of students from that course. Michael Collins, as the course director and primary lecturer, brings to this book a wealth of information, while Benjamin Scott brings his experiences of putting that theory into action. Within two months of finishing Michael's course, Benjamin had beaten off over a thousand applicants to win a prestigious job in advertising. Michael Collins is also an interviewer for Norfolk County Council.

We would like to thank our publishers, Giles Lewis and Nikki Read, as well as all the staff and sales teams at How To Books.

We would also like to thank Jacqueline Stead, Stephanie Yule, Rachel Spencer, Chris Lee, Peter McConnell, Tom Vick, Dave Waters, Ash Makkar and (an extra big thank to) Jacqueline Wyatt for some excellent photographs.

Thanks also to the anonymous (but brave) donors of their winning CVs and covering and speculative letters.

Introduction

The fact you are reading this sentence suggests you are halfway to making the transition from student to career person. Planning your career-building strategy is not rocket science; in fact, most of it is that very uncommon thing – 'common sense'. There are two basic points to remember when reading this book:

1. Getting that dream job is usually achieved by not being eliminated from the selection process, rather than by a flash of divine inspiration.

2. The system works.

Use this book to suit your own circumstances. Read it from cover to cover or dip in and out of it as you feel you need to. And, while you're reading it, be thankful there are still people who can't be bothered or who thought their natural charm would win the day. At least they've already been eliminated from the race.

Remember, job-hunting *can* be a daunting process and most recruitment processes are not fun or user friendly (they are, after all, there to help the company, not you). But don't let fear of rejection and fear of getting the job stop you. Just go for it.

TIME

There is always too little time, but don't think that skimping any time from your job-hunting will help. The more time you spend preparing (researching, writing applications, etc.), the less time you will spend looking for a job because each application will be that much more effective. So devote some time to it. Every moment you spend working on an application brings you that much closer to your dream job.

A WARNING: CAREER VERSUS JOB

You do not want a job, you want a career. Anyone can have a 'job'. You've probably been using jobs to get you through university. Unless you are making a conscious choice to be flipping burgers or stacking shelves for the rest of your life remember this – a career is different from a job. A career includes promotions, raises, bonuses, more involvement with a company and more satisfaction. Most graduate interviewers want to hear that you're planning a career, that you have ambition and that you want to succeed (and to help their organisation or company succeed too).

HUNTING FOR GEMS AND BUILDING YOUR OWN 'BULLSHIT ANTENNA'

There is an endless number of books, websites and people who are willing to offer you advice. There are even so-called experts who are willing to charge you for their advice. Some of this advice will be useful. Some of this advice will be useless, damaging or simply just expensive.

Free advice is always worth listening to although not necessarily worth following. Always listen out for 'gems':

those little bits of information that make you think, 'ah, yes, there's something in that'.

With the rest of that advice out there, you need to realise quickly that some of it is complete guff and nonsense. You need to equip yourself consciously with a 'bullshit antenna' so you can differentiate the bad ideas from the good. Think about who is offering you the advice: why should you follow *their* advice? How reliable is it? How does it fit in with the other information that you have gathered? Are they trying to manipulate you to their own ends?

Part one

Before You Start Applying

$$\left(\,1\,\right)$$

Making a Confident Career Choice

WHAT DO YOU WANT TO BE WHEN YOU GROW UP?

Such an easy question to answer when you were aged between 5 and 12 but, now, panic sets in when you're asked: 'What are you going to do after your degree?' The question hasn't changed but your answer has. You're now aware that the world is bigger, brimming with possibilities. Your basic career choices have now expanded beyond 'happy families', beyond just fireman, baker, nurse and soldier. You have goals and expectations for your entire life. You don't want to fail, to make a wrong decision and be stuck in a job you will hate for ever.

Don't panic. At this stage all you need to decide is what career you would like to try first. It is unlikely you will have a single career for your whole life – as we will discuss in Chapter 4, you will probably have four or five careers, each one more rewarding and enjoyable. Whatever you choose now will not stop you doing something different in five or ten years but should increase your confidence and your skills.

Making an informed choice and knowing about the career you want will make the job-hunting easier. You can then throw away the job ads and start tackling companies directly, cutting out the competition and the laborious recruitment processes. You can use your friends and families to help find the right position for you, and companies might even create a new post for you.

But, first of all, you need to work out what your ideal career will be. This chapter has a number of 'self-analysis devices' (or thinking exercises) to help you make the choice. The results will also be useful as raw material for your CV, covering letter and interview preparation.

MAKING A DECISION

> *I am nearly 60 and I still have no idea what I want to do next.* (Michael Collins)

There is no disgrace in not knowing what you want to do as a career. In fact, if truth were told, who really knows? After all, there are thousands and thousands of career options – just look through the Careers Library Classification Index (CLCI) or a careers directory (or even the good-old *Yellow Pages*). One difficulty in choosing a career is that the more options on the menu, the harder it is to choose one. You need to find out what sort of job you will enjoy and be good at.

There are no 'perfect' jobs (i.e. ones that are all joy and no tears). Every job has its downsides as well as its ups. When we talk about your dream or perfect career, what we really mean is a career that suits you. In other words, one you will enjoy so much you can forgive the downside. And you'll only really know if you made the right decision when you actually do the job for real, so don't worry about making a wrong decision – go for it and see what happens.

GUT INSTINCT EXERCISE 1

Step 1
Brainstorm (write down) all the careers you can think of.

Step 2
From your original list, separate out the careers into two lists – ones you don't even want to consider and ones that tempt you. Don't worry if one list is longer than the other – you're trying to narrow the fields you are considering.

Step 3
Go back and number each career in order of how strongly you feel about them (i.e. which do you hate the most and which do you fancy doing the most?).

Step 4
Now look at the top-five careers on each list and think about why you've said whether you hate/love the idea of doing that career. What makes you think you'll love/hate, be successful/unsuccessful in each career? Are there any common features on those lists?

Step 5
Make a note of your observations.

GUT INSTINCT EXERCISE 2

Step 1
Brainstorm a list of things you love, from ice cream to the way people act around you to traits in people you admire.

Step 2
Brainstorm a list of things you hate, again from the very small things to the bigger things.

Step 3
Try to write down a reason for each thing on the list. Highlight those you feel strongly about or which give you some sort of clue about what jobs you would like to do, or would hate to do. For example, perhaps you hate computers because you prefer dealing with real people. Your instincts might tell you that a career as a computer programmer isn't the best option, but a management or customer focused role (even within ICT) would be a better option.

Or, if you love public speaking because you like explaining things to people, you could look for careers which involve either making lots of presentations (perhaps sales or lecturing) or counselling (from finance (an IFA) to personal issues (a Relate counsellor)).

THE 'WHAT YOUR PAST CAN TELL YOU' EXERCISE

Employers judge potential by past performance. They assume that, if you were successful before, you'll be successful again. For example, employers looking for 'management material' will invariably seek out candidates who have leadership roles on their CVs (i.e. captain of the football or hockey team). This exercise, therefore, does the reverse. It will help you look at your past to see what it might suggest about your future.

Step 1

Write down all the qualifications you have. Jot down every exam you've passed and every certificate you have, from a Duke of Edinburgh award to your degree. Write down where you got them as well, from the Scouts to university.

Step 2

List the following things:

- Jobs you have done for other people (paid or unpaid).

- Other things you've done (charity fundraisers, sponsored walks, drama productions, etc.).

- Your interests (hobbies, favourite TV programmes, books, captain of the netball team, etc,).

Use words that also describe the skills you used in doing all these things – did you *write*? *Produce*? *Negotiate*? *Help*? *Organise*? *Manage*? *Participate*? *Sell*? Use every verb (i.e. doing word) that comes to mind.

Step 3

Rearrange all the information into four lists (you might want to use a separate piece of paper for each list):

1. *What you enjoy doing:* Which skills do you enjoy using? What are your favourite subjects? What do you have the fondest memories of doing?

2. *What you least enjoy:* Which skill do you hate using? Which subjects were you glad to have finished or, plain hated?

3. *What you're good/best at:* What are your strongest subjects? What stands out as your great achievements?

4. *What you're not good/worst at:* What were your weakest grades (if any)? What activities have you done that were just failures?

Step 4

Highlight everything that is on *both* the 'enjoyed doing' and the 'were good at' lists. These should help suggest careers that are worth investigating. Some will be obvious as a career option (for example, your first-aid course might suggest a career in a medical field or for a charity). Other options won't be so obvious but there are exercises later in Chapter 2 that might help you find these hidden career options.

Step 5

Now look at things that are *both* on the 'hated' and 'weren't good at' lists. Depending how strongly you feel, you probably want to avoid careers that feature them – so watch out for them when investigating any careers options.

PUTTING ALL THE RESULTS TOGETHER

Look at all the results from all three exercises. You should now be able to rule out a number of careers, either with good reason or from gut instinct. More importantly, you should have a list of careers that are worth exploring. You can use the next chapter to help you round out these ideas and to explore new ones. Chapters 5, 6, and 7 can help you investigate these options as careers.

2

Considering Other Directions

Having thought about what sort of job you'll enjoy, it's time to look at other factors that might influence your career choice. Write down your thoughts and reactions as you work through this chapter.

GEOGRAPHIC PREFERENCES

You need to think about the following issues:

- Are you willing to relocate in order to pursue a particular career?
- Are there areas of this country that you would not be willing to move to?
- How far are you willing to travel every day?
- Are you prepared to work abroad?

Any of these factors could either limit your search to companies and industries within a 10–20 miles radius of your home or could expand your job search to the global village (particularly for more specialised fields where opportunities in a single country are limited). Be honest with yourself: if the location doesn't suit, why put yourself through the time and trouble of that job search?

EDUCATIONAL FACTORS

Your degree has opened up opportunities that are not as readily available to people without degrees. A flick through the *Guardian* job section shows that many companies only want to consider graduates. However, your degree might not be the minimum level of education needed for your dream career. For example, a university lecturer now requires a PhD for a permanent post, teachers require a PGCE (Postgraduate Certificate of Education) and accountants take years of exams to become qualified. So:

◆ Given your current education and career ambitions, are your current qualifications enough to follow that particular career?

◆ More importantly, if not, are you willing to pursue further qualifications?

◆ If you are willing, will you have to pay to become qualified or will a company/the state pay for you?

MORAL/SPIRITUAL PREFERENCES
Without getting too New Age, you should also consider moral or spiritual implications of careers. Service industries such as marketing and advertising may have clients who sell tobacco or use animal testing. A career in biological research might lead you into embryology and cloning research. So, be honest: do you hold any strong beliefs that would stop you working for a specific company or industry?

MOTIVATIONAL FACTORS
What do you really want out of your career? Okay, you don't want a career you'll hate, but what do you really want out of your career?

- Is it purely about the size of reward? How much money you can make or how much holiday you'll get? Do you just want enough money to live? Or do you want enough money to take loads of foreign holidays, or to buy a house, or to follow your ideal lifestyle (for example, having a pet, or buying new shoes every month)?

- Do you want to change the world? Do you want to know that you've made a difference above just receiving a material reward?

- Is it about satisfaction? Do you just want to be proud at the end of the day with what you've achieved? Is it about competition and ambition? Do you want to work in an industry that makes it easier to judge your performance against someone else?

- Do you want a high-profile career? Something that either gives you fame or recognition (either within the industry or with the general public)?

- Do you just want a career where you can use and develop your favourite skills?

- Or do you have a passion or obsession you want to pursue regardless of anything else?

RISK PREFERENCES

While there are no certainties or jobs for life, some careers are still more stable and secure than others. Ask yourself how you feel about the following:

- *High-risk occupations* (including industries with high staff turnover, that are quick to shed jobs in bad times or that are based on 'project work'). These occupations might include, for example, high-pressure, high-reward jobs (like stockbroking), freelance and consultancy work, self-employment, start-ups/expanding companies, new sectors, or other off-beat careers.

◆ *Low-risk occupations* (usually established or essential sectors with clearly defined structures and a stable number of employees – although there are never any guarantees). These occupations might include, for example, the public sector (including councils, schools, hospitals and the Civil Service) and 'blue chip' or FTSE 100 companies. Looking carefully at the company history helps you judge its stability – is it keeping up with the competition? Is it expanding/ shrinking rapidly?

OTHER FACTORS

What are you prepared to do for your ideal career, and what are you not prepared to do (both in the short term and long term)?

◆ How much extra work are you willing to put in? Are you willing to work outside normal office hours or do anti-social hours?

◆ How much physical exertion can you put in?

◆ Are you prepared to do any public speaking? What about working on your own? Or working in a close team?

◆ What are your future plans, and how will your career fit into these?

PULLING EVERYTHING TOGETHER

You should now have a list of the key elements of any ideal job. If you can name the career or field you want to explore, start researching. If you can't name the job but know the sort of skills you want to use, start talking to people. Ask everyone you know (friends, relatives, teachers, etc.), if they know which jobs would use those skills – 'I am looking for a job that uses X, Y and Z skills. Do you know of any jobs that might benefit from these skills?'

You can also do a bit of 'random' career hunting:

- Look through the material and books available in the careers section of a library and in careers centres.

- Browse the Internet, or even the *Yellow Pages*, for ideas.

- Read the job ads in newspapers – cut out any ad that might be suitable or sounds attractive. Explore those jobs and find out what careers in that area involve (then go after the companies that didn't advertise).

Or if you just want to start earning while you make up your mind, try a temping agency. You'll get to experience a range of work environments to watch people in an assortment of jobs. This can help you decide what you will want to do and perhaps more importantly what you definitely don't want to do, as well as boosting your CV with new experience, skills and training.

MORE METHODICAL WAYS TO FIND A CAREER TO PURSUE

If you still don't know what you want, don't despair: there

are other sources of help you might find useful.

Computer programs

There are plenty of careers software packages that take
your preferences and turn them into concrete suggestions.
You might have used something similar at secondary
school or sixth form college. Most of these software
packages take about half an hour to an hour to use, and
they give you your results in the form of a prioritised list
of job titles and careers.

Of course, these programs are not gifted with any special
abilities; they use preset parameters and, frankly, the
machine doesn't care who you are or know anything
about you. They are not oracles and cannot see what the
future holds. Their answers are advisory – suggestions of
possible avenues. The final decision is yours.

Your careers centre should have a couple of machines
with some sort of career guidance software on them, and
access is usually free. If you don't have access to a free
software package, you might want to try an Internet-
based package (e.g. www.learndirect.co.uk) or pay for one
as part of a service provided by a paid careers consultant
or county careers service (all in *Yellow Pages*).

As a final word about these software options, they are
useful to help focus your mind or to come up with new
suggestions. If you can do one for free then do so;
otherwise, think carefully before paying for the service.
Whether the answers are from the result of research or a
psychologist's recommendations, the results are still only

preset answers, limited to your input and the size of their careers database. In other words, you might be ideally suited to be a teacher except for the fact that the machine didn't know you hate children.

This applies to the numerous and patented systems that use psychological preference as a means of careers advice. These tests can be an invaluable insight into your mind and are invaluable for personal/career development, but as careers guidance devices we are not convinced. They can make helpful suggestions, but they don't take into account other motivations such as your experiences, dreams and fears.

Careers advisers

Some people think highly of careers advisers – especially the ones to whom they paid good money. After all, the emperor paid handsomely for his new clothes and thought them wonderful. Whatever you do, start by considering their service cynically. Quiz them about what they are going to do before paying any money. Know what you're getting for your money. And don't just speak to one – research several advisers before making your pick to find the one that's best for you. In most cases the finest careers adviser is the person looking back at you in the mirror.

3

Skills You Bring an Employer

Why do companies want to employ graduates? Let's face it, few jobs, if any, really require a degree to do them. Despite this, many professions have 'entry criteria' – usually a set number of qualifications that are 'recognised' as proof of ability. The medical profession (particularly doctors) is a prime example, but do you actually need a medical degree to diagnose illnesses? No, you only need one to be allowed to practise as a doctor. You certainly don't need a degree to become an innovator, a successful business person or even a pillar of the community.

Few careers, except academia, actually require the knowledge learnt during a degree. Yet many of the jobs ask specifically for graduates – not because they need employees who can discuss the merits of Virginia Woolf or the dissemination of heresy in southern France but because you spent the last few years learning and developing 'transferable skills'.

WHAT SKILLS?

You have transferable skills. You started to develop them as part of your degree. They're generalised skills that can be used in a series of different environments. The exercise that follows will help you understand what skills you can offer a prospective employer. It will help you write CVs, covering letters and application forms. It should also help you to explain concisely to an employer why you are the best candidate for the job.

Don't worry about which skills you write down: include everything you can think of. The end product is for your eyes only. Don't forget to add to this list whenever you remember those skills you accidentally missed off the list or when you learn new ones.

Step 1
Take a look at the list below and write out all the skills you have that are on that list. Then add any skills you have that aren't listed:

- Listening and taking notes.
- Finding and organising information.
- Writing reports and essays.
- Managing your time.
- Working to deadlines.
- Gathering and organising information.
- Analysing and interpreting texts, visual images or data.
- Understanding abstract concepts.
- Explaining abstract concepts or complex events (orally or in writing).
- Empathising with other people, understanding their motivations or points of view.
- Comprehending how and why other cultures differ from your own.
- Distinguishing between various types of causation.
- Imagining alternative scenarios.

- Collaborating on group projects or participating in group discussions.
- Computer (information communication technology) skills: from wordprocessing and using the Internet to email and using databases.

Step 2

For each of the skills you have, try to break them down into smaller sub-skills. For example, essay writing could include the following:

- Researching, investigating, questioning.
- Organising, planning, prioritising.
- Problem-solving, analysing, lateral thinking.
- Writing, summarising.
- Explaining, persuading.
- Discussions (with tutors, experts or fellow students).
- Tenacity, determination.
- Reading, library skills.
- Using ICT (from using the web to wordprocessing your essay).

Step 3

Think of the skills you have gained outside your degree. These could be things you do for a hobby, a university society, a part-time job or something you did before you came to university. For example:

- Organising skills (creating publicity, chairing meetings, negotiating bookings).

- Secretarial skills (filing, taking enquiries by phone, ordering stationery).

Step 4

Review your list of skills and pick out five skills you enjoy doing and five skills you are good at so that you have a list of ten key skills. Compare your ten key skills with those from Chapter 1. Do they match up with the career paths you were considering? Are there any alternative jobs that combine all your favourite skills? Which skills or experiences mean the most to you? Which skills would you really miss using?

WHAT EMPLOYERS REALLY WANT: A WORD OF WARNING

Employers want transferable skills, which is why your degree subject is usually *irrelevant* to most career choices. What you bring to the employer is the ability to learn and develop your skills in the way the company wants. After all, you're only beginning to develop these skills – a good thing considering they are going to retrain you anyway, de-programme your university learning and teach you about how real business works.

So, what else are employers after? Unsurprisingly, the typical graduate doesn't start a career in the board-room but in the photocopying room. This is because what employers really want from most graduates is a good 6–18 months as a slave, doing menial tasks without complaint. In some industries this is seen as a rite of passage, the 'we-went-through-hell-when-we-joined-so-why-shouldn't-you' mentality. In other industries it is seen more as a learning experience. Graduates are often fast tracked to 'management' so they need to have experience of every level in the organisation. After all, a good manager never delegates something they would not be prepared to do (or have done) themselves.

There are other skills employers are after and therefore look out for during the interview process:

◆ People who can add value, who do extra things that are not necessarily part of the job descriptions. For example, people who will volunteer to come and help at the weekends (for no extra pay, perhaps?).

◆ People who take the initiative and organise things without being asked.

◆ 'Fixers not finger pointers' – in other words, people who take responsibility for a situation that has gone bad by finding a workable solution.

◆ People who are fully committed to the job while they are at work. People who do not organise their social lives or run their hobbies in company time, especially if there is work to do.

◆ People with the ability to accept ambiguity and uncertainty, and with a willingness to change working practices and skills as required.

◆ Graduates who are willing to keep on learning, developing and pushing themselves further.

◆ And, finally, people who hold themselves accountable to the outcomes of their actions.

IDENTIFYING THE SKILLS AN INDUSTRY DESIRES

Your success will come from a targeted approach to employers, finding out exactly what they want and then delivering it. If an employer needs someone who can crunch statistics, you need to tell them you can crunch statistics and then prove to them you can (it was part of your degree course/worked with statistics for a summer job, etc.).

To analyse the skills an industry/job requires you will need to look at the following:

◆ Job ads, job descriptions and application notes (for the jobs you're interested in).

◆ Company websites and corporate literature.

◆ Any 'guides to', or articles about, working in that industry.

◆ Notes from any conversations you've had with people who do that job (see Chapter 6).

Just like an essay, look at your sources or evidence (such as the examples listed above) and try to pick out the key information. This process can be broken down into three steps.

Step 1
The real basics. Take everything at face value and start compiling a list of skills that are required (for example, communication skills, a background in a retail environment, a keen interest in ICT or fluency in two or more languages). As best you can, differentiate the skills required by an industry/job/company between:

◆ *compulsory/prerequisite skills* (i.e. you must have those skills to be considered); and

- *advantage/desirable skills* (i.e. the very best candidates might have these).

Step 2
Read between the lines: what have your sources/evidence implied?

- If a firm talks about a company car, they probably expect you to be able to drive (either for business or just getting to work because of their location), so you add 'driving skills' to the compulsory list.

- Talk about a dynamic and fast-paced environment might mean time management skills, an ability to cope with change, an ability to work on your own and an ability to meet short deadlines.

- Annual commission structures or a genuine desire to achieve beg the question: are you ambitious? Are you likely to push yourself hard for rewards? Can you solve problems and see new opportunities?

Also keep an eye out for anything else that may influence your decisions to approach that career. References to flexibility could be a coded reference to late hours, lots of travel or the need to relocate.

Step 3
Compare your skills and experiences with those required by the jobs: are there any you lack? Can you get away without having them – in other words, are they prerequisites? Of course, if you have all the skills they are asking for, make sure these are reflected in your application or CV and covering letter.

GETTING THE SKILLS YOU WANT/NEED

Transferable skills come from many sources. You might need to go after specific skills in order to meet the criteria or to set yourself apart from the competition. For instance, if you want to be a journalist you do not need a Media Studies degree, but you will need shorthand. Ask yourself before committing yourself to anything (especially if parting with money): if I pick up skills this way, will it be recognised by an employer? Is there another way into the industry that doesn't involve having that skill as a prerequisite?

◆ *University societies.* This is easy if you're still at university. Team sports are great for teamwork skills, and most societies have committees and official positions that need filling (e.g. being treasurer of the Music Society gives you those important numerical skills as well as giving the impression that you are a 'doer', a person of action and responsibility).

◆ *Voluntary clubs/societies.* There are also lots of public clubs and societies outside university, from your local pumpkin-growing club to writers' circles, reading groups, single-issue action groups and even political parties. Membership fees are usually small, and most probably have a couple of official positions to fill which could provide those skills (check your local public library, local council website or local press for details).

◆ *Courses.* More education might be the best solution but will probably cost you money. Your university and your local college are a good place to start, as is www.learndirect.co.uk (tel: 0800 100 900). Ask yourself: will this course be recognised by an employer as useful? If you're in any doubt, ring someone in the industry and ask.

- *Voluntary work/work experience* (see Chapter 6).

- *Paid work.* In an ideal world you should be able to get paid to develop new skills, but it is difficult to find a job that will give you the opportunity to pick up the skills you need. You might, therefore, have to start by being paid less than you expected but, with a cunning career strategy to hand as well, you'll soon get to the position you deserve.

- *Take a year out* (see Chapter 9).

$$\bigcirc\!\!\!4$$

Having the Courage to Follow Your Career Choice

Choosing your own career path can be unsettling. It's even tempting to let other people, such as your parents or careers advisers prescribe a career path for you. Don't. You are the creator of your career goals: only you know the dreams you want to follow. Don't worry if you are not 100% certain about a particular career – it's still worth exploring. Nothing but your own experience can tell you if an industry is right or wrong for you. So get your foot in the door and then decide.

Go for the career you think will make you happiest; this usually turns out to be the most successful approach. The excitement and determination from following your own plan might be that 'special spark' which swings an application, or interview, in your favour. Be confident – the question facing you is not whether you can get a job, but which job you take and in which particular industry.

YOUR PARENTS' ADVICE

My parents offered me more advice than I could handle. They wanted me to join the army or get a safe job with the council. Instead, luckily, I filled in an application for a multinational oil company that my parents never even

> *knew existed. Mum and Dad had never considered I wanted to work abroad.* (Michael Collins)

Your parents should not be trusted where your future career direction is concerned. Their advice, however well intended, is tempered by their own experience and desires. Nine times out of ten parents will try to persuade you into a career you will hate and perhaps even one that does not exist. Worse still, their advice may even prevent you from getting the job you really want. Remember the following:

Parents are not infallible or experts

Unless directly involved in a recruitment process, your parents will have little or no knowledge about job-hunting for *graduates, today.* Besides, your university experience has developed and nurtured you as an adult. It is this self-reliance rather than your degree certificate that makes you attractive to employers. Your ability to think independently was hard earned: don't throw it away.

The world has changed

The world of work and the opportunities within it are continuously changing (even as you read this book). Your parents will not be aware of all opportunities that are open to *you.* If they are graduates, the world you face is different from the one they faced when they left university. In the past, employers fought over university graduates. With over 30% of the school population gaining a degree (a figure growing every year), employers are now spoilt for choice. What you need now is a degree *and* a strategy (an 'angle') to make the best use of that piece of paper from your university.

Parents like safe careers options

Blame genetics, which seek to protect the next generation from harm. Your parents want to see you happy, but they also want to avoid having to support you financially any longer. To fulfil these mixed desires they will have a definite idea about which career path you should take. This might be any old job (especially where paying off those loans is concerned); it might be a specific career (the usual clichés about doctors, lawyers and accountants); or a few may want you to follow in their own footsteps. When it becomes hard to separate their desires from your own it is time to be passionate about your own agenda – the one you devised. Remind them, and yourself, it's your life: you have the right to make your own mistakes and successes.

MAKING YOUR PARENTS USEFUL

No matter how your parents react to your career choices, they remain an integral part of your social network. Their contacts and knowledge about a particular industry may be invaluable. Even so, be aware that they will probably offer very different advice to you than they would to a client or friend. Photographing crocodiles along the Nile may well be a great experience for a colleague to acquire but it will not be recommended for an offspring carrying their own reproductive genes. So, grab any nuggets they offer but judge each suggestion carefully before using it.

Don't forget that you control the information your parents receive about your career plans. Be careful what you tell them. To make life easier, consider creating a strategy to manage your parents. Here are three ideas:

1. Avoid asking for, or inviting, their advice. (In theory, the best move but, in practice, it is probably inviting a relationship disaster.)

2. Share your plans – explain your goals, convince them you have done your research and planned ahead. (This is the best course of action, if you are up for it – and great practice for interviews too!)

3. Do not challenge their advice but secretly follow your career plan. (A dubious solution but, sadly, sometimes the only way.)

CAREERS CENTRES

Do not avoid the careers centre if you have access to one. They can be an invaluable resource, giving you access to information/people that could save a lot of time and effort. But, like parents, careers advisers (and such like) come with **a big, bold health warning**. Careers advisers, of all shapes and sizes, are usually lovely people with great intentions but remember that their first priority is not to you, it is to themselves and their job. Only you know that dream lurking in the far recesses of your head.

True, most want 'the best' for you, except that 'the best' comes wrapped in their experiences, not yours. They may well want to solve your 'lack of prospects' problem and will invariably suggest career choices where there are a readily available number of jobs – i.e. large employers (e.g. whoever is the biggest in your area/near your university/London) or big professions (e.g. teaching or the Civil Service). Extract information from them, listen to their advice and then use it for your own purposes.

Always decide for yourself if you want to follow any advice offered to you, and even then filter everything through your own personal 'bullshit antenna'.

THE MYTH OF AN INDUSTRY THAT'S HARD TO ENTER

Everyone told me it was difficult to get into the advertising industry, especially with a history degree. To be honest, it made me even more determined. Despite all the hard work, countless interviews and positive thinking, it was still a major shock when I was finally offered a job. Now I know nothing is impossible, if you have determination and a strategy. (Benjamin Scott)

Never be put off by the generic label 'an industry that's hard to enter'. This usually refers to the more glamorous and creative industries, such as advertising and entertainment. It is undoubtedly true that every industry has its bright, super-intelligent individuals, but no industry could ever survive without a majority of normal people who do the work – people like you and me. But this myth still puts many people off even considering applying. This is good news for you as it whittles down the competition.

With a bit of planning, research and self-presentation (plus a little bit of luck), you can get almost any job you want. However, job-hunting is not a spur-of-the-moment activity. If approached with careful planning, like a military campaign called 'operation career' and executed to the best of your ability, you will succeed. What have you got to lose? Are you frightened of a little rejection or that you actually may just succeed?

NOT LETTING FEAR OF FAILING HOLD YOU BACK

The big career-hunting secret is: *just have a go*. Without taking risks we do not grow as individuals, and the time for taking risks is right now while you are resilient and young enough, as the song says, to 'dust yourself down and start all over again'. Be prepared for failure; it is how most people learn. It tells us what we don't like doing and what we do like. And it is that experience that makes us more attractive to employers because it develops us and our skills. So get out there and give it your best shot!

NO LIFETIME COMMITMENT TO ONE CAREER ONLY

Don't feel overwhelmed in making a choice of career. Whatever decision you take now – even if it is wrong – can be changed. All you are choosing is where to *start* your working life. Take comfort in that, no matter how well you research and choose your career and employer, you will probably be working in a different organisation within three years. In fact, if you're not, most employers will think you probably lack ambition. In ten years or less you might be working in a completely different industry, even one that does not exist today.

Your degree creates flexibility and choice to deal with the constant change in modern life. It opens the doors of opportunity into most professions. Change is inevitable; sometimes we initiate it, when we tire of a job or an industry, sometimes it is forced upon us by economic circumstances. So it's always worth having half an idea of what you might like to do next.

Whatever happens, give whichever industry you choose your best shot. You may even be super lucky and find the job you really enjoy, a.k.a. the perfect job, first time. But remember, this is only the beginning of your working life and probably the first of a variety of satisfying mini-careers.

Once employed, take at least six months to decide whether a new industry is right for you. If nothing else, too many very short stays in a series of jobs will look bad on your CV. If you do leave early, your next employer will want to know why. One to two years is the optimum time to evaluate any job or industry. You will be ready to shake off those final parental shackles and make a hole in those debts. Professionally, you will no longer be the 'new person'. You will have more experience and will have learnt new skills or developed old ones that will make you 'hot property'.

And whenever you do decide to 'stay put' it will not be because you feel you cannot get another job but because you are well on your way to that meteoric rise to the top. And you did it all yourself.

(5)

Researching Your Career Choices

Hard, basic research is part of nearly every degree. For every essay, seminar and exam you collect information from a variety of resources, including lectures, seminars, talks with your tutor, textbooks, the library and the Internet. Given that every graduate has done some research as part of his or her degree, it is not surprising that most interviewers become frustrated at applicants who do no research, particularly as employers are not stupid – they know how easy it is to find out information about their company and their industry.

Think about it: why spend all that time and effort applying for a job and going to an interview when you don't know what you're getting yourself into? Researching your potential career will help you to:

- decide what career options you want to follow;
- understand the industry you're going to work in;
- open up new opportunities (hopefully!);
- write/tailor a confident application, CV and covering letter; and
- sparkle during your interviews and get you that job!

REAL KNOWLEDGE IS POWER

The more you know about an industry/job before applying, the more confident you will appear to the interviewer. Your methods of research are relatively unimportant as long as the sources of the information are reliable and you process that information through your 'bullshit antenna'. The following are just a few of the methods you could use.

✓ *Work sampling* – i.e. work experience or shadowing (see Chapter 6).

✓ *Ask people to talk to you* – most people love to talk about themselves.

✓ *Libraries* – public, university and specialist.

✓ *Careers centres* – public and university (even if you've already graduated, many university careers centres allow ex-students/the public to use their resources, although they may charge).

✓ *Books* – a range of materials from job-hunting to self-help guides specific to an industry (i.e. *Starting and Running a Café* or *Working in Television*) to corporate histories and books by captains of industry (e.g. *Ogilvy on Advertising* – Prion, 1995), and even to critiques of an industry (e.g. *Fast Food Nation* by Eric Schlosser – G.K. Hall, 2001).

✓ *Newspapers* – broadsheet newspaper business sections (sometimes even the main section). Also valuable is *The Financial Times*.

✓ *Trade magazines* – every industry has one, from nursing (*Nursing Today*) to advertising (*Campaign*), from plumbing and heating (*PHARM*) to publishing (*The Bookseller*).

✓ *Company annual reports* – downloadable from company sites or free to order through www.ft.com.

✓ *Websites* – most companies now have their own websites loaded with lots of yummy information. Check out competitor sites and search newspapers and newsgroups. If you have time, spread the net wider with a search engine or two.

✓ And, if you're willing to pay, there are plenty of companies who'll do the research for you.

WHAT TO FIND OUT

General questions

The following are some general questions you might need to answer in relation to a particular industry:

◆ What are your expectations of the industry? Does the industry actually match up to those expectations? Is the industry right for you?

◆ What could you do? Are there any jobs that appeal to you?

◆ How do people normally get into that industry? What are the exceptions to that rule?

Specific questions

The following are more detailed questions you might need when researching further into a specific industry:

◆ What are the general trends for that sector? Is it expanding, stagnant or declining?

- How is the sector structured? How do they make a profit?

- Who is doing the firing and hiring? Who are the market leaders, the big players and the new kids in town?

- Have there been any mergers recently?

- What does success mean for that industry (i.e. big contracts, awards or profit)?

Questions about a specific company

Finally, the following are questions you might need when researching a specific company:

- What is its niche? What makes it different from its competitors?

- What do they like to talk about? What do they actually do? What are they proud of? (Look at their website or annual reports.)

- What sort of business is it? A partnership, a plc, a family-run business? Is it listed on the FTSE?

- In what direction are their shares heading?

- Latest news. (Have they just expanded or won more funding?)

- What do other people say about the company? (News reports, other entrepreneurs, ex-employees or customer grievance sites.)

◆ If you want to become a teacher. Investigate a school's catchment area: What type is it? What are the kids like (working class, middle class)? Is it an area of high unemployment? What about the school's league table position? Check out www.upmystreet.com.

TALKING TO PEOPLE (BUILDING AND USING YOUR NETWORK)

People are the most valuable source of information you have about an industry. Everyone loves to talk about him- or herself – especially if we have a willing and interested audience – and most people welcome an opportunity to talk about what they do for a living.

You need to find someone who is doing the job you want. The chances are that you already know someone who does. If you don't, perhaps someone in your network does. Just think of all the people you know: your family, friends and acquaintances. Now, think of all the people they know: their friends, family and acquaintances. Remember, your network is not just the people you know but the people they know. For example, your flatmate's dad might be a barrister or his uncle might be a heating engineer; or your mum's hairdresser's husband could be an accountant. Asking around, especially if you have strong, positive self-branding (see Chapter 8), can find contacts in the unlikeliest of places. Remember, at this stage you are just fact-finding; do not ask for a job or a recommendation. Let them decide whether they want to recommend you, or tell you about a vacancy when it appears. Of course, nothing in life is free. Always offer to buy them a coffee, drink or lunch to discuss their career.

And be prepared to do something for them – find out how you could help them.

Don't despair if your current network is failing to provide you with any decent contacts. Try to think laterally; is there anyone who deals with the industry you are planning to go into? For example, if your uncle is a printer he might deal with publishers on a daily basis. Perhaps he can tell you his impression as an outsider or even find a contact for you. Write to people you don't know (using *Yellow Pages* and a telephone) and ask them if they can spend 20 minutes talking to you about their job. As most people love to talk about themselves, it's quite easy and, although not everyone will make the time, many will.

USING YOUR RESEARCH AT INTERVIEWS

Treat every company you apply to as special. After all, you want a job with them. Develop a list of sensible questions to ask at the interview. Review your notes – what strikes you as particularly relevant to the future of the company or your job with them? Make sure all the questions are relevant to that company. Write questions on a pocket-sized piece of card so that, when the interviewer asks you 'do you have any questions?', you can pull out the card and ask them. It will show you are prepared for the interview and will leave a good impression. (And don't forget to write the company's name on the card so you don't ask the wrong questions at the wrong interview.)

Don't be afraid to ask about anything you didn't understand in your reading. This can be a useful way to highlight the fact that you did some reading/research (i.e. I read that your company was formed out of a merger two years ago. What were the reasons behind that decision?).

Remember, pay attention to the answers. Use body language to show that you're listening (nodding, eye contact, etc.). Respond to the answers – perhaps follow them up with another question – to show that you care about the answers.

A final tip: on the way to the interview, read the financial section of the newspaper or the relevant trade press. Keep an eye out for a story about the company you are going to see. Add any topical questions – what are the reasons behind the latest movement of their share price? Or how are they affected by new legislation or recent economic indicators?

(6)

Test Driving Your Career

Work experience allows you to explore different career paths without having to sign up to a job. It doesn't matter if you have a vague notion or a firm vision of your perfect career, work experience will still help you to:

- decide whether a career path is right for you;

- provide fantastic ammunition for interviews/applications;

- gain insider information about who is hiring, how they are hired and whom to approach;

- gain invaluable application and interview practice; and

- give your CV an 'edge' over other candidates for the real job.

Work experience comes in several forms:

- *Formal work experience programmes.* These usually involve larger companies in industries that have a history of students asking for work experience. These programmes are normally tailored to students and take place over the summer and Easter holidays, occasionally with notional pay.

- *Informal work experience*. Smaller companies (and some larger ones) often have no formal programme or procedure. It's usually up to managers/bosses to consider applications on merit and workload (nepotism and doing clients favours also play a big role). Time and pay, if any, are usually by negotiation. These are usually 'work placements' – one to two weeks unpaid.

- *Summer work*. Many firms look for temporary staff over the summer holidays.

- *Work shadowing*. Following someone around for a day, or perhaps a week to learn about his or her job, etc.

- *Paid work*. Part-time, temporary or agency work – probably likely to be administrative, perhaps secretarial, paid (of course) and offers the opportunity to find out about 'backdoor' opportunities – plus you get to check out a variety of industries in a short space of time.

- *Voluntary work*. Picking up skills and experience and the opportunity to make a role 'yours'. If you want to go into the charity/socially conscious industries, a commitment to good works is probably a prerequisite. Besides, most companies/interviewers admire charity work (it impresses!).

- *And, finally, just talking to people on the inside*. Not strictly work experience but a valuable source of information which could, if played correctly, lead to work experience or a job.

OBTAINING WORK EXPERIENCE

The process of asking for work experience is exactly the same as applying for a job but it is made easier because the majority of companies look at work experience requests more favourably than 'pleas' for a job. So, the simple answer is to create a CV, ring up the company and send them a letter. Another method is to write asking for advice first and then follow up an information interview with a work experience request.

Don't lie to yourself that you don't have time to do work experience – make time! Work experience should be a priority. Be prepared to work for free for a couple of weeks (within reason). Remember, they're doing you a favour, not the other way round, although good employers should offer to reimburse travelling expenses (but don't count on it).

And don't forget to utilise your network (see Chapter 5) to get work experience. Companies who never accept students on work placement are often willing to do so as a favour for a client or employee but be warned: you'll have even more to prove if you go down this route.

FINDING INSIDER INFORMATION

During your career test drive you need to find out as much as you can about life in that industry. This insider knowledge can be used to evaluate whether the industry really represents what you want:

♦ Can you earn the money you thought you could?

♦ Are you going to be able to use the skills you wanted to?

- What do people really love and hate about their jobs?

- What is a typical week?

- What makes people stay or leave that industry?

- How do people turn up for interviews? What do they ask them? What answers are they looking for from applicants?

- How do people normally enter the industry (e.g. graduate recruitment programmes, through agencies or mainly speculatively)? What are the exceptions to the rule?

- What skills will you need to obtain the job you want? What skills will you need to get the promotion to the level after that?

- What is the industry structure (i.e. who are the bottom and who are the top)? What do the job titles mean? How do people enter the industry and how do they get on? What sort of jargon is used?

- What is the gender mix of the industry? Is there a 'locker-room culture', and could you cope with it?

Once you have gathered this information and used it to make your career choice, you can recycle it into brilliant interview answers. For example, consider the favourite interviewer questions: 'Why do you want this job?' and 'Can you do this job?' By using your work experience as an example you can show you understand something about the industry and how to do the job. It can also show your ability to set goals, to plan ahead and to research.

Work experience can really make a difference as it demonstrates one of the hardest things to prove: your passion and enthusiasm for a career. Few employers will expect or even believe that your work experience was a constructive and fulfilling experience. They know you made endless mugs of tea and did a mountain of photocopying. But the fact that you actually put up with it shows you're motivated and hardworking (and this certainly counts for more than the difference between a 1st and a 2:1 to most employers).

AVOIDING JOBS YOU'LL END UP HATING

Work experience, in all its forms, can help you find the real pitfalls of an industry. Now is the time to find out those things that potentially make it a career from hell. For example:

◆ Social work – can you deal with such issues as incest?

◆ Veterinary work – could you kill a suffering animal?

◆ Lecturing – are monetary rewards worth the long hours?

◆ Journalism – are you prepared to question people who have just lost a loved one in order to get the story?

◆ Emergency services – can you cope with violent or horrific deaths?

By talking to people in these industries before you enter them you might discover other issues you never before considered. And if you still want to follow that career after learning the downsides, share that decision in interviews: it'll be fantastic ammunition. After all, there is no better answer to 'why do you want this job?' than 'because I did some work experience and decided that it was the best career for me. I wanted to do X, Y, and Z and feel that I can cope with A, B, C'. Amazing!

Remember, there is no such thing as wasted work experience. Even if you hated it you can still use it to argue effectively about why you want to go into one industry rather than another.

GETTING WORK EXPERIENCE TO WORK FOR YOU

Work experience on your CV also does much to reassure your potential employer. Look at the world around you and you'll realise that students have a bad reputation: promiscuous lager louts, drug-taking hippies and people who can't get out of bed before noon. Few employers, if any, will accept that you worked hard at university. They may be graduates themselves, have kids who have been students or might just have a stereotyped image of students. Your work experience will help destroy these preconceptions by giving you credibility, while some of your competition (fellow students and graduates) will undoubtedly fall into the trap of confirming the worst of these stereotypes.

University clubs and societies also provide excellent evidence for your CV. In particular, student newspapers and radio stations provide an invaluable 'body of work' for media-related careers, especially journalism and copywriting. Being a treasurer or chair of any society will enhance your CV regardless of the career you're pursuing. If you're lucky enough to read this before the end of your final year, rush out and join some societies: get a position on their committee and make useful suggestions. Or why not start a new society?

If you still have a summer or two left before you graduate, be warned: employers will ask what you did during your long university summer holidays – temporary work is fine, interesting, voluntary or 'different' work is brilliant, but doing nothing could be damaging.

Finally, remember to treat work experience with the same professionalism and determination you will show in your main job hunt. Impress your bosses enough and, you never know, they might even ask you to stay.

7

Building a Cunning Plan (with a fiendish backup)

You now know that you don't just want any old job, working in any old industry. You are aiming for a specific job that will help you develop and use the skills you want to and, at the end of the day, give you a sense of satisfaction. What you need now is a plan or a strategy that will outline how you are going to achieve your goals. The advantages of having a 'cunning plan' are clear – it will keep you focused on your goals and help you manage your motivation. It will include a 'plan B' to use if one particular route fails to help you achieve your goals. And, most importantly, it will increase your chances of getting the job you really want.

A CASE STUDY

This case study is true, although we have changed the subject's name. Debbie wanted to work in the auction industry. The graduate recruitment schemes she investigated all required a first in fine art, and she only had a 2:2. Determined to follow her dream, she joined a temping agency and asked that, if any opportunities to temp inside an auction house came up, she wanted to do them (but was happy doing the other stuff in the

---

mean time). Six months later, she got her dream as-signment in a well-known auction house. And when the secretary she was covering for decided to leave, she was asked to stay.

A year later Debbie was able to take advantage of a junior position that had suddenly become vacant. Her hard work paid off and, since then, she has continued to rise through the company doing exactly what she set out to do.

WHAT YOU WANT OUT OF LIFE

Work isn't everything although it will be an important influence on your life. You need to have your own personal goals: dreams that motivate you, things that make you strive that little bit harder. Once you decide what you want out of life, planning your career (and working) becomes easier. Suddenly, getting that dream career has a reason:

- ◆ Is it fame or fortune?

- ◆ Is it to have enough money or experience to set up your own business?

- ◆ Is it perhaps to have expensive holidays in exotic locations, or the latest fashions or a fast car?

- ◆ Or, perhaps, you want to raise a family or buy a house?

Set yourself a time limit but be realistic: when will you achieve these goals? Is it in the next five, ten or even twenty years?

WHAT IS YOUR CAREER GOAL?

Where do you want to start your career(s)? Why do you want to work in that industry? How will it help you achieve your personal goals? Put a time limit on this – i.e. after ten years working in this industry I want to own a business, or in five years I want to be professionally qualified, etc. For example: 'I want to work in advertising because I want to be involved in the creative process and utilise my problem-solving skills. I also want to earn enough money to buy a house within the next ten years.'

GETTING THE JOB YOU WANT

Developing a successful strategy (i.e. one that *works*) depends on outlining options and alternative routes as backup if one fails. It makes sense that, if you approach a job from two different angles you have a higher chance of succeeding than if you only had one approach – i.e. just responding to a newspaper ad, as opposed to replying to the ad and writing to another company speculatively. So, ideally, you should try to use at least two methods in order to reach your goal. Don't use every method at once but have a plan (and write it down, even if it's just a list on piece of scrap paper) that you can refer to when your current methods aren't working.

Give each of your options a time limit for them to work (depending on your circumstances, a couple of months per option is the minimum time you should allow). Some you'll want to continue using, although you might want to change the amount of energy/effort you use following those leads.

There are two basic approaches to getting a job:

1. Using the front door – the hardest but most obvious route (i.e. recruitment programmes and advertisements).
2. Using the back door – a less obvious route but more successful (i.e. speculative letters, temping, work experience and short-term contracts).

Front door: graduate recruitment programmes

It is unsurprising to hear that these programmes are on the decline. It is an expensive and time-consuming route, favoured particularly by big industries, such as accounting and management, in order to keep the numbers of recruits entering the industry at a stable level. To put cost into perspective, a graduate hired this way costs at least three times his or her yearly salary. This money is spent on glossy brochures, websites, advertising, time spent sifting through CVs and interviewing candidates, paying expenses and training once a candidate has been selected – an almost endless list of costs. Many companies also join the 'milk round' tour of *selected* universities and careers fairs to promote their programme.

It is easy to find these programmes by looking at company websites, the leaflets and information in your university careers centre (including bulky graduate 'catalogues') and by asking the associations and societies that represent that industry. These programmes are an obvious first port of call for you as well as the thousands of other candidates, as the schemes offer a fast-tracked approach to your career. It goes without saying that it is tough (but *never* impossible) to be recruited this way.

A CASE STUDY

The following is also true but, again, the subject's name has been changed. Alex was due to graduate with a history 2:1. At the beginning of his third year he decided he wanted to go into advertising. After re-searching the industry using a careers library and the Internet, he speculatively approached industry insiders who advised him to choose between a job as a creative or as an account handler. The route to becoming a creative involved additional and expensive qualifica-tions, plus up to four years of low-paid work place-ments, so he decided the account-handling route would be a quicker way into the industry. He applied to a dozen graduate programmes for London advertis-ing agencies. The company that hired him had over a thousand applicants, who were quickly whittled down to two employees using four rounds of interviews and assessments. Hard work, but worth it.

Front door: advertisements

Newspapers, job centres and university careers centres are all sources of recruitment advertising, as are 'job search sites' on the Internet. These ads are placed by companies willing to spend money trying to find new staff, so it would seem silly not to answer these calls.

However, while the numbers of people applying for these jobs vary from position to position depending on the industry, you could easily be competing against thousands of hopefuls. There will also be additional recruitment devices used to help 'weed out' the majority of candidates.

Back-door methods

Back-door methods are great because they can help you bypass not only the competition but also, sometimes, all those recruitment tests. You may be nervous using these methods as they tend to be less formal and 'secure' as the front-door method, but they do get results.

What we mean by back-door methods are:

- bespoke recruiting or speculative applications;
- work placements;
- work experience;
- opportunities produced by your network;
- recruitment agency work; and
- part-time or temporary contracts.

All these may sound like slave labour but they are great opportunities. The competition is focused on full-time/ permanent positions through traditional front-door methods. This leaves the 'back-door route' open to you. It'll be easier to 'get in' and, once there, you can be ready for the next permanent vacancy by having already demonstrated your abilities on the job. You can also decide whether the company or job is right for you before committing to a long-term contract.

Back-door methods are also popular with employers as they reduce the cost of recruitment (both in time and money). These methods also increase the chances of finding the right employee because they have seen you in action. The fact that you have actually worked there, and still want to sign up, shows your dedication to the company.

Every industry has different back-door/side-door methods of recruiting. For example, design-orientated industries hire freelancers to test their performance before offering lucrative contracts. Ask people you contact the following questions:

- How did they get their career in that industry?
- How are people normally recruited? What are the rules and, more importantly, what are the exceptions to those rules?

WRITING DOWN YOUR CUNNING PLAN
Remember:

- Try to have more than one approach to that dream job.
- Make sure you know what you could do if things don't work out.

EXAMPLE: A REAL-LIFE CUNNING PLAN

Goal: 'I want to work in advertising because I want to be involved in the creative process and utilise my problem-solving skills. I also want to earn enough money to buy a house within the next ten years'.

1. 'London agency' graduate recruitment programmes (account handling).

---

2. 'Client-side' marketing recruitment programmes.

3. Speculative approach to local/regional advertising agencies (account handling or creative).

4. Work for recruitment agency, asking for temporary jobs in advertising agencies (keep building CV and repeating steps 1–3).

5. *If* no success after four months (or longer if getting interviews) do training in web design and plan for Internet/interactive opportunities.

8

Developing Your Own Brand

'So who are you?' This seems a stupid question – of course you know who you are. But do you really know yourself and, more to the point, can you put into single words your personality, aims, hopes, strengths and weaknesses? If you can, you have either done an exercise such as the one that follows before, or you should really get out more.

The idea you will be selected for a job or a promotion solely on the basis of your qualifications or experience ignores a key part of human behaviour: our emotions. Nearly all decisions in life involve some sort of an emotional element, from buying shoes to selecting an employee. These feelings, positive or negative, will impact on you and your application.

Sometimes, for better or worse, these feelings can be instinctive and unconscious. The employer's reaction might be 'I don't like the look of him' or 'I don't know why but I just don't like her' or even 'I must have that talent working for me'. When this happens, there isn't anything you can do.

However, the majority of the time you do have influence over other people's reactions because you control what they see, hear and read about you. Companies such as Coca-Cola, Shell or Diesel spend millions every year trying to influence consumers' feelings about their brands. These emotional messages sometimes outweigh such practical considerations as value for money or usefulness.

Every application, interview and, most importantly, contact with your network is an opportunity to get your brand across. Managing your brand can bring many benefits:

◆ New opportunities because no one will hesitate in recommending you or being associated with you.

◆ Writing applications and answering interview questions will become easier because you'll understand yourself better and be more in control.

◆ You can take advantage of the emotional side of the hiring process, hopefully convincing employers you're a 'must have'. It also makes interviewers feel they can recommend you (i.e. you won't embarrass them by being a bad choice!).

DECIDING ON YOUR BRAND

Your brand is your name or reputation. It's the feelings people associate with that name (e.g. 'She works so hard', 'I'd never trust him', 'He takes everything so calmly' or 'She's so lazy!'). It's up to you to convince others of the real you by demonstrating your brand values (not by arguing, unless you want to be seen as argumentative and unreasonable). Remember, the aim of self-branding is to *convince others* they can feel proud of recommending you for the job/interview. Use the following exercise to help you recognise and develop your own brand.

BRAND VALUES EXERCISE: WHAT DOES YOUR BRAND (i.e. YOU) STAND FOR?

This is an exercise to help you discover/refine your brand. It only requires 30 mins to one hour to do, a piece of A4 paper, a pen and a thesaurus (the fatter the better).

Step 1

Write your name in a box in the middle of the paper and then draw ten lines out of the box.

Step 2

Write at the end of each line a word you think describes you – try to be as positive as you can. It's best if you do this off the top of your head, but, if you struggle, look at what you wrote for the exercises in Chapters 1 and 2. (If you're brave enough, you could even ask a friend what he or she thinks your strengths are).

Step 3

Using a thesaurus, look up each word. Write down the five most appealing words listed. They can be the most accurate descriptions of you, ones that just sound good or even ones that you aspire to.

You should end up with something that looks like Figure 1.

Step 4

Choose the ten words that best apply to you and to your chosen career (circling them with a different colour helps). To make life easier, we are going to refer to these ten words as your 'brand values'.

For example, Benjamin did this exercise with becoming an advertising account manager in mind (which explains 'odd ball'). The brand values he chose are enthusiastic, resourceful, enterprising, problem-solving, tenacious, organised, different, helpful, quirky and professional (a substitution for reliable).

Step 5
For each brand value write down evidence of how you have demonstrated it, or how you could demonstrate it. For example, enthusiastic could be demonstrated by the fact you are strong supporter of a university society or did a lot of extracircular activities at school (such as plays, etc.).

USING YOUR BRAND
Refer to your 'brand values' (and the chart from the exercise) whenever you are writing an application or preparing for an interview. Use as many of your ten words as possible when writing a covering letter or application form. Take 'enthusiasm': it could be used directly ('It was my enthusiasm and organisation that enabled me to make a success of the History Society's publicity campaigns') or indirectly, ('I am very *keen* to enter the advertising industry which is demonstrated by my work experience at...').

Always use proof to back up your brand value. It sounds rather lame and flimsy just to say 'I am enthusiastic'. Anyone can say 'I am hard working' but few people will remember to back it up with an example.

This branding exercise is also useful for interviews. One very common interview question, particularly for graduate positions, is 'choose five words that best describe you' or 'choose five words which your friends would use to describe you'. Luckily, the exercise has already given you the answer. Indeed, you have enough words for two different answers, so tailor your answers to the company/position.

Don't forget, the first time an employer will have sustained contact with you will be through the written word: your covering letter, CV or application form. These are the best opportunities to establish your brand. The words you use can have a subconscious influence on the reader – so use them to your advantage!

MORE BRAND TRICKS: PUTTING SPIN ON BAD NEWS

We all have parts of ourselves which we would describe as weaknesses – things we know deep down are probably bad things (i.e. being too shy, too talkative, etc.). In politics, the term 'spin doctoring' is given to those people whose job it is to put a positive twist to bad or unfavourable news. You can do the same for yourself. For example, if you're shy or introverted, you could call yourself 'quiet' or a 'deep thinker'.

Think about controlling other aspects of your brand, including:

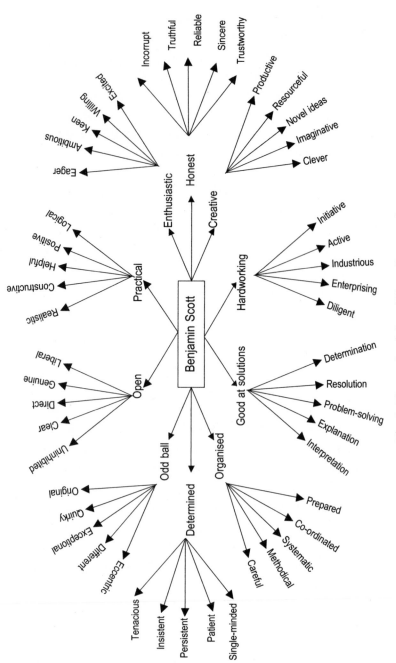

Fig. 1. The result of the self-branding exercise.

- How you dress and act.

- Your answerphone/voice-mail message (and signature on emails).

- Where you answer your mobile phone – taking an employer's call in a pub during the day time destroys the credability of your claim to be hard working.

TURNING YOUR NETWORK INTO BRAND AMBASSADORS

If your network (your friends, family and acquaintances) is going to open the doors to new opportunities, you need to convince them you're worth recommending. The trouble is that most of these people will see you at your weakest. Show them you're worth recommending (or hiring) and you then have an additional path to follow in your job hunt.

Remember, your aunt (or anyone in your network) could be at a party and be talking to an employer who is desperate to fill a vacancy (your dream job even!) but, having only ever seen you nursing hangovers, she refuses to mention your name and changes the subject. After all, it's her reputation that's at stake too.

INFORMATION ABOUT YOU ON THE WEB

Without being vain, search the Internet for information about yourself – using search engines. It's amazing what you might find, from Uncle Albert's family photo album (pictures of you aged 8) or photos of the rugby team's summer party, to a chat room devoted to your fraudulent use of society funds, etc. If you find negative references ask the website owner to remove them. It will be just as easy for an employer to search the web and find those references as it was for you. It might even be time to close down your long-forgotten 'I want to be Barbie' website (unless, of course, you're going for a job at Mattel).

(9)

Supercharging Your CV
with a Year Out

First the bad news: taking a year out after graduating may
not be the best thing to do for your career. In effect, you'll
be losing your place in the recruitment queue and once
you return a year older, you'll be competing with
thousands of bright-eyed, eager and fresh students who
have just graduated. But if you can't resist the temptation
of taking a year out and discovering the world, there is
good news. With a little planning you can make a year out
work for you. It can supercharge your CV so that, when
you do come back, you're in a prime position to launch
your career.

Remember, the majority of year-out advocates have their
own agendas which do not include helping you to build a
successful career. These include the following:

♦ *The travel industry* – magazines (whose income
  depends on advertisers selling holidays and insurance),
  travel companies (who want to sell you plane tickets),
  insurance companies (because only a fool would
  backpack without some form of cover) and, finally,
  authors and publishers (who want you to buy their
  travel guides and maps).

◆ *Last year's graduates* who, after taking a year out, realise that they have missed the boat and want to rid themselves of unnecessary competition for this year's jobs.

◆ *'Fellow traveller types'* whose enthusiasm for international communism should be warning enough: they don't like to see anyone working, full stop.

Take a year out because you really want to do something, not because you want to supercharge your CV. If it has been your lifelong dream to explore New Zealand, discover China or to wonder through America's purple mountain majesty, then brilliant, go, because a year out is about the personal experience. And you'll have an amazing time.

CONVINCING EMPLOYERS OF THE VALUE OF A YEAR OUT

It is hard, almost impossible, to convince most employers that a year out is anything other than for personal pleasure. They tend to see graduates who have taken a year out to globe-trot as 'work shy'. Even living in India for six months or backpacking through South America, does little to raise your employment prospects. You can still be viewed as lacking any real experience – in particular, experience of business.

Many employers are suspicious, if not a little jealous, of backpacking students. You have had a freedom they don't have: freedom from responsibilities, freedom from real hard work and freedom from routine. For this, many are prepared to brand you a 'feckless hedonist'. So when the question comes (and it will definitely come), 'why did you decide to take a year out?' answer carefully. The honest answer is that you went because you wanted to backpack around Vietnam to get it out of your system before having to settle down and take on the responsibilities of being a working adult.

Don't be tempted to say that your year in Australia shows a new-found maturity and self-reliance, making you a model potential employee. Many employers will view your experience differently. They will have seen the TV programmes and newspapers exposés on 'British students abroad'. Their expectation will be that you spent your time working in bars, drinking beer, chatting up the local talent and getting tanned (in both senses). This perception gets worse with years out spent in anywhere closely associated with clubbing or drugs. Just watch them raise their eyebrows before crossing your name off the list.

PUTTING YOUR YEAR OUT TO GOOD USE

Having said all this, spending a year out wisely can help supercharge your CV, so when you return you'll be ahead of that newly graduated competition. To do this, you need to make sure that you spend your year *picking up new skills, not just picking fruit* – in other words, adding value to your CV.

Let's face it, most travellers go for sun and enjoyment and they do it in English, but if you can learn a new language or improve an old one you've got it made. Even though English is an international language, the majority of the world doesn't speak it as their first language. Some of the best languages to learn are Spanish (useful for South

America, Mexico and the USA), Portuguese (the language of Brazil), French (spoken in many African countries), German and Chinese. And before you swoon at the thought of verb tables and vocabulary tests, we are not talking A-levels but a working use of the language: being able to book a hotel for your boss or read an email from a foreign-speaking client. It's easy to be lazy abroad as so many people now speak English, particularly in tourist destinations, but if you try your best to learn the local language it could help you land your dream job.

Whatever you do during your year out, the only way to impress employers is to show that you did something using your brain. You want your year out to improve your 'brand', to give a good impression on your behalf and to show employers some IQ. These days it's nothing special to travel abroad. Travel programmes have demystified exotic holidays, making potential employers as interested in your year out as you would be seeing their holiday snaps. So in order to make your experience count for you, surprise them – they will be expecting leisure and low-wage activities: lazing on the beach, climbing through mountains, picking fruit. But think how impressive it will look if you spent your time doing something useful, such as work in an Australian bank for a few months or teach English as a foreign language (which, by the way, could lead to an additional qualification and a whole new avenue of employment opportunities).

You can also use a year out to demonstrate responsibility: again, anything beyond the normal 'leisure'-styled year out. For example, going to Ibiza isn't impressive but going out as a club rep is (although how much more impressive is up for debate). Teaching abroad is another brilliant opportunity (and a great way to see real life in foreign countries, particularly those where there are two sides to the country – i.e. the tourist side and real life). There is also a plethora of organisations offering volunteer work aboard, ranging from VSO (Voluntary Services Overseas) to Camp America. Even the UN offers opportunities abroad.

AN ALTERNATIVE SUGGESTION

Why not consider just waiting? Get your career started first and then, once you have a couple years of experience working in the real world, take a year out. Surprisingly, a lot of employers are far more tolerant of employees who take a break to see the world than people who do so before even starting a job. The rise of maternity leave and career breaks for mothers (particularly in high-level positions) has made it harder for many employers to refuse staff the right to take lengthy unpaid holidays and sabbaticals. There is also an amount of admiration for staff willing to sacrifice pay and other benefits in order to follow their dreams. This admiration only comes, of course, to people who have something to lose. And, as an additional incentive, you'll have saved some serious amounts of money that will make the trip, and reintegrating back into society when you return, a lot easier (plus you'll have those two, or more, years of experience on your CV).

Part two

Applying

The Undoubted Power of Speculative Letters

The amazing figure that up to 70% of job vacancies are never advertised is why speculative letters are undoubtedly powerful. The competition for each job will be dramatically reduced, from hundreds to no more than a dozen. And, before an employer even looks at your letter, you've already demonstrated your 'get up and go'.

Speculative letters and covering letters serve the same purpose – to get you an interview (which in turn leads to a job). Both letters sell the skills you have to offer to a potential employer and stress the link between you and what the job/company requires. They should persuade the reader you are the ideal candidate; the only difference should be that your speculative letter is going to an employer who has not advertised for your services – it, therefore, has to work harder on that one side of A4.

All CVs should be accompanied by a letter. Not only is it expected but it is also an opportunity for you to sell yourself. After all, the employer can only go by what **you tell them**, and a letter opens the dialogue. A poor covering letter will cause your CV to go straight into the bin without even being read. This applies equally to emailing

CVs to people (although we recommend you don't, unless asked to).

Always include an SAE with a speculative letter or a letter requesting an information interview/work experience.

WRITING A BRILLIANT LETTER: THE BASICS

Always wordprocess your letters, unless specifically asked not to (for tips on handwritten letters, see Chapter 14). Put your name, address, telephone number and email (if there is room) in the top right-hand corner. Underneath your details put the date you're posting the letter. Don't use computer-generated letterheads – they will distract from your message.

After your details, put the details of the person you're writing to on the left-hand side, including his or her full name and title (i.e. Mr John Smith) and their job title (i.e. Managing Director), followed by the company's name and address.

'Dear sir/madam' is lazy and should not be used unless totally unavoidable. All it takes is one minute to phone a receptionist or secretary to ask about someone's name and job title – simply writing to a specific person will increase your chances of success.

WRITING A BRILLIANT LETTER: THE CONTENT

Remember, you are demonstrating your ability to write a concise business letter and your ability to write persuasively. Before you read any further, think about what questions an employer will have when reading your letter.

What will impress them? What will they want to know? Your letter must answer their questions, particularly:

♦ Why do you want a career in that area?
♦ Why this company?
♦ Do you have the skills and attitude for the job?

A letter can be broken down into four parts: an opening, an explanation, extra information and, finally, a positive ending. Don't forget to use the words from your self-branding list as well as action words (i.e. verbs or doing words) and to demonstrate your enthusiasm.

An opening
You need to explain why you're writing. If you are responding to an ad you need to say where you saw it (i.e. *Guardian*, Monday 3 March 2003). When writing speculatively you need to tell them what sort of position you are interested in. It's always better to apply to specific jobs/areas. Your research should have revealed to you a good starting job, and don't forget to use the language of the industry – don't be an outsider.

If you're in any doubt, ring them (or a similar firm) and ask what positions they recruit graduates into. The worst thing that can happen is they say no. Remember, you're not just thinking about becoming an X: believe your future *is* in X.

If you can slip in a reference to a company achievement, do. It might be the reason why you want to work for them (i.e. an award or industry poll) or the reason why you are writing to them (i.e. an expansion). Tailor the letter specifically to the company and job, and don't be afraid to show that you know something about their organisation – it'll help your letter stand out.

Don't forget to mention you've enclosed your CV.

An explanation

You now need to explain why you're the most suitable candidate for the job. Outline the skills, strengths and experiences you bring to the job. In other words, sell yourself. Give them a persuasive argument why your application should go forward to the next round. Highlight the great things on your CV – in particular, your work shadowing, work experience, enthusiasm and, most importantly, your transferable skills.

Use your research to cover each of the main skills you think, or know, they are looking for. Don't forget to use evidence to support your claims (i.e. 'being the chair of the debating society has helped me to develop my verbal communication skills, which will be valuable when talking to clients').

If you're responding to an ad, cover everything it asks for.

Extra information

Make sure you tell them any key information they need to know. If there is anything in your CV that might concern the employer, pre-empt any shortcomings by pointing out the potential problem and why it is not really a problem (e.g. there is a gap on your CV but you did learn X, Y, and Z during that period).

You can also, if you're being sneaky, answer questions you know they can't ask you (for example, by adding 'I do not have any commitments that will stop me from travelling' you're reassuring them that you are mobile). If you know there might be driving involved (a company car in the ad is a clue), add that you have a clean driving licence or are about to take your driving test.

A positive ending

Remind them you are eager to hear from them and/or looking forward to having an interview with them. If you think they might be really busy, you could offer to phone them in a week (as long as you do!).

When you finish a letter always sign off 'yours sincerely' ('yours faithfully' only if you are forced to write to 'Dear sir/madam') followed by your signature (use a fountain pen if you can) and your printed name. You can vary the ending if you wish – for example, 'Warmest regards', 'Best regards' or 'Yours hopefully'.

FOLLOWING UP LEADS

If a contact recommends that you write to someone he or she knows, always follow up the lead – it is expected. Then, reference your contact at the beginning of the letter (for example, 'John Smith, who worked with you at X Company, recommended that I write to you about working at Y Company'). Out of courtesy to the person making the recommendation, make sure you have his or her permission. Send that person a copy of your letter to let him or her know what you said (and so that he or she will be impressed enough to recommend another opportunity).

If you get a good response from a speculative letter (i.e. a positive no-thank-you-at-the-moment), follow it up again in two to three months' time, especially when you have something new to say (you've graduated, done more relevant work experience, finished an evening course, moved house, etc.). Usefully, you will also know whom to write to as this person wrote a reply to you (or were mentioned – i.e. 'the head of engineering doesn't have any vacancies at the moment...'). On no account give up: positions fall vacant all the time, and they can only say no.

A CASE STUDY

As before, the following is true but we have changed the subject's name. Amber wanted to work in market research. She wrote to about fifty or so companies speculatively and got a handful of positive but unsuccessful replies. She followed up six letters she felt were particular good replies every two months. On her third letter to one of the companies, they asked her to come in for an interview and offered her a job.

EXAMPLE LETTERS

We have included three example letters (Figures 2, 3 and 4). They are not perfect but they are *real letters that worked*. We have, of course, changed the names and the companies but largely left the letters as they were (even though there are things we would do to improve them). They cover:

- writing for work experience;
- writing for a job speculatively; and
- responding to a job ad.

Don't forget, once you've written your letter think about how it appears on the page. Does it look cluttered and confused or neat and professional?

Another Person
First Line of Address
City
Postcode

9 October XXXX

Mr Arthur Fictitious
Partner
Disguised Company
First line of address
City
Postcode

Dear Mr Fictitious

I am a final year undergraduate at UEA determined to pursue a career in advertising. I am writing to you in the hope that I will be able to gain some experience and insight into the industry, either through shadowing or direct work experience.

I believe that I have the personal qualities, and the basic skills, to make either an excellent account manager or copywriter. However, I need to learn how the industry operates, and thus gain experience. I do feel that it is crucial to talk to established people within the industry for their views and experiences. I have already had some experience with amateur efforts in fields closely related to advertising, namely in magazine and film production.

As part of my degree I am currently taking a course run by Dr Collins, on Personal and Academic Development, with a heavy focus on professionalism, presentation and team-work skills. I feel that my enthusiasm and eagerness to learn will be of benefit to anyone that gives me an opportunity to work, for however short a period.

Once again could I stress my eagerness to enter the industry, and I hope that you can offer me help, either with advice on entering and succeeding within the industry. Or, better still, an invitation to speak to you personally and possibly allow me to visit your company to gain an insight into daily operations.

I really would like to take this opportunity to thank you for taking the time to read this letter and look forward to hearing from you shortly.

Yours sincerely
Another Person

Fig. 2. Speculative letter: work experience.

Another Person
First Line of Address
City
Postcode

2 April XXXX

Miss Random Fictitious
Partner
Disguised Company
First line of address
London
Postcode

Dear Miss Fictitious

I am a final year undergraduate who is determined to pursue a career in market research. I am actively working towards obtaining the necessary skills and experience to make an excellent Research Executive, although I am willing to take on most positions to make a start in the industry. My work at XYZ Research has fired my enthusiasm, and introduced me to, a career in market research.

My enclosed CV outlines the skills and experience relevant to positions in market research. I would particularly like to highlight:

♦ analytical skills, demonstrated by my landscape archaeology project which involved analysing a wide variety of sources and large amounts of data. This particularly included using my numeracy skills and computer literacy.
♦ problem-solving ability. As a history undergraduate, essay writing involves a high element of problem-solving and analysis. In particular presenting solutions persuasively, weighing up options and coming to conclusions on controversial issues.
♦ team-work and communication skills, through being in a band and doing group projects at university. During my work as a telephone interviewer and at Anytown College, I have developed my oral and written communication skills. As a student adviser it is essential to take an interest in the students assigned to me, as I am responsible for their welfare.
♦ ability to organise and plan. As a member of the University History Society committee, I am constantly using these skills to organise events both academic and social.

From August I shall be moving to London, although I can move earlier if necessary. I do look forward to hearing from you, and discussing further what I can offer Disguised Company.

Yours sincerely
Another Person

Fig. 3. Speculative letter: work.

Another Person
First Line of Address
City
Postcode

2 April XXXX

Mrs Fictitious
Human Resource Officer
Disguised Company
First line of address
London
Postcode

Dear Mrs Fictitious

I am applying for the position of Research Executive as advertised in Research magazine on the 21 March XXXX. My enclosed CV outlines the skills and experience relevant to this position. I would particularly like to highlight:

♦ analytical skills, demonstrated by my landscape archaeology project which involved analysing a wide variety of sources and large amounts of data. This included using numeracy skills.

♦ attention to detail. History, as an academic discipline, requires strong attention to detail, especially with regards to citations and statistical evidence. It also requires the ability to structure work coherently and communicate effectively. This skill is being developed further by my dissertation, which demands higher levels of planning, organisation and problem-solving.

♦ work as a telephone interviewer. This has provided me with experience of using questionnaires both on CATI stations and on paper, including pointing out mistakes and problems on questionnaires used, which have been rectified as a result.

♦ computer literacy. I am competent using wordprocessing packages, such as Word, and am familiar with administration tasks through my work at Anytown College.

♦ team-work and inter-personal skills, through being in a band and during a group project for a university module. My work as a telephone interviewer is further developing my oral communication skills. As a student adviser it is essential to take an interest in the students assigned to me as I am responsible for their welfare.

I am determined to pursue a career in market research. Therefore I offer you my energy, enthusiasm and dedication. Working as a Research Executive for a company that has been leading independent market research for 30 years will be invaluable in developing my skills to be successful in the industry. I really do look forward to hearing from you soon and discussing my application further.

Yours sincerely
Another Person

Fig. 4. Covering letter: work.

(11)

Stopping Your Application from Going in the Bin

Remember, for every application, the best candidate has already been binned. Despite having the right skills and experience and something extra that could contribute to the organisation, the ideal candidate has already been put in the 'no thank you' pile. An underpaid secretary or work experience student has added the candidate's details to a standard 'thank you, but no thank you' letter and, most likely, no one has even read or looked at the candidate's application for more than a couple of seconds.

Of course, it depends on the employer. But few companies or organisations have the resources to examine every CV and application form thoroughly or to interview every candidate for a job. So, they sift down the applications to a manageable size. Companies do this by discounting candidates they think they don't want. In other words, at every stage of the sifting process, your challenge is to avoid being binned.

Employers receive hundreds, if not thousands, of letters a year and, to be fair, they have to somehow sort through the piles of CVs and application forms. So they start by just binning applications that fail to meet their expectations. The initial stage isn't even about content, it's about the basics. Did you get the name right? Does it look attractive? Are there any obvious spelling mistakes?

There is an urban legend (and it doesn't even matter if it's true) that during the 1980s a London finance company used to throw all the applications (unopened) down a flight of stairs, reading only those that landed at the bottom.

Obviously, sometimes there is nothing you can do to stop them binning you. But there are several steps you can take to reduce the risk:

- Read any instructions carefully, and make sure you follow them *exactly*. If it says 'black ink' then assume any other colour will be binned.

- Use first-class post – sometimes companies will bin 'second class' post.

- Never fold your application or CV and covering letter. Always use an A4 envelope – either white or cardboard backed (fold your CV and send it to yourself if you don't believe us).

- Always print letters and CVs on good-quality white or cream A4 bond paper with a watermark (avoid coloured paper as it is hard to read, scan, and photocopy).

- Use a laser printer or a good-quality inkjet; never use a dot-matrix printer.

- Never use scented, flowery, hole-punched or lined paper.

- If there is a reference number on the job ad or application form then put it on the top left-hand corner of the envelope.

- No tea/coffee-cup stains, food splashes or odours (imagine opening a garlic or fried-food smelling application!).

- Make sure everything you send looks professional and business-like.

Assume that 50–60% of candidates disappear at this stage. Luckily for you, the competition has now been dramatically reduced – fewer people stand in your way to that dream job. But you're still at risk as they reduce the pile further.

Imagine it's your job to sort through a hundred applications, or perhaps even a thousand. The sheer size of the task is daunting. You only really want to interview at most fifty candidates for each position available. So, after binning 50% of the applications, what's next? Well, because the recruitment process is time consuming, companies use lower-paid workers to sort through CVs – it's just cheaper that way. Some companies even use electronic CV readers, which reduce costs even further (see Chapter 13). Whichever method they use, the strategy is the same: bin the applications that fail to meet the basic criteria.

Your application will be compared to basic prerequisites for the job. If it requires a clean driving licence and *you haven't said* you've got one (or planning to get one), you're out. If the job requires two language skills and you've not said you're fluent in Russian and German, you're out. If the job requires teamwork and good communication skills, you need to say explicitly 'I have teamwork skills as demonstrated by...'. Remember, the person sifting through your CV is doing a job and that is to bin as many applications as possible. It is up to you to make it clear you have the skills needed for the job to stop that person from binning you.

Once you've escaped these hurdles, your application is then examined in detail as preparation for interview. Obviously, this process is not the same for every company, but even a small company that gets a speculative letter once a fortnight can't invite everyone who writes in for an interview. They will still sift through the application against the same issues. If your application looks poor (or like a bulk mailing) they won't ask you for an interview. Don't cover the basics and it doesn't even matter what you've written.

Read through everything you send carefully – at least five times. Proofreaders often recommend reading through things backwards to spot spelling mistakes – do it at least once. Watch out for the ending of the words – is it in the right tense? Have you got the right word (incite or insight, roll or role)? Ask a trusted friend to check things for you – they might spot the errors you don't.

Make sure everything written is relevant to that company. Make sure that reference to another employer hasn't crept in (this is possible if you're using an old letter as a template).

Always send things to a real person. *Ring* up and ask. Confirm you have spelt that person's name correctly and that his or her job title and personal title are correct (Mrs, Ms, Miss, Mr, Dr, Sir, etc.). Be extra careful with unisex names, such as Jo and Alex.

IF YOUR APPLICATION IS BINNED

The successful (and brave!) job hunter will ask companies for feedback if his or her application is binned. Not many companies are prepared to do this (again, the scale of the task is a deciding factor) but, if they offer to give feedback on application forms, take it! You never know, it might even be a test to see if you are willing to take criticism and willing to find out why things didn't go right. If it was a speculative application you might ask if it was your application or their circumstances that was the deciding factor. Just tread carefully, remain cool and be prepared to hear things you don't want to hear.

$$\left(\widehat{12}\right)$$

Don't Be Afraid of the Big Bad Application Forms

APPLICATION FORMS

Application forms are deliberately written to put people off. Employers create them for their own ease of use, not yours. They are another administrative device employed by employers to thin down the number of applicants. Take up the challenge and fill in the form. An advertising agency, notorious for its 'creative' approach to application forms (as most of the industry is), managed to cut down the number of applicants from over 2,000 to under 500 by making their application form more demanding. For the brave who filled in the form (including sending in various personal objects), more than half were interviewed – their enthusiasm for the job and the industry was unquestionable.

GUIDELINES FOR COMPLETING APPLICATION FORMS

Making sure you do everything required

Do as you are told. Follow any instructions carefully – most companies get enough good applications to bin those that fail to follow the instructions. Don't be tripped up by silly mistakes. Even if the application asks for a tape of you making animal noises, as one company once did, still do it. Let other people put themselves out of the race by giving up.

Photocopying the form before you start

Get four copies so you can draft out your answers to make sure they fit the boxes. For the computer literate, some forms can be printed over (depending on the paper they're printed on and the capabilities of your computer). This is hard to do well and a very risky procedure, especially if you only have one copy of the application form. Mistakes do happen. I once printed out an application form and messed up one page of it. Luckily the form was plain black and white, and I had a spare copy of that page that I could stick carefully over the ruined page. Risky, but I still got an interview either because they didn't notice or they liked my resourcefulness.

Giving yourself the time to do it well

Resist the temptation of doing everything just in time. Give yourself the opportunity not only to prepare properly but also ample time once the form has been completed to check for errors or to take action if disaster strikes (for example, if you spill tea over the form and need a new one or you break your writing hand). Phoning the company for a new application the day before the deadline will not leave a favourable impression.

Creating your answers, or filling in the form

The form is only part of the process, not the end result. Someone will still have to read and judge your application. Again, should you be asked in for an interview? Do you meet all the criteria? Will you add something to the company?

Just like cover letters, speculative letters and CVs, you need to tailor your answers on an application form. So, do your homework:

- What is the position you're applying for? Are there any prerequisites you need to highlight?
- What skills are they looking for?
- What attitudes or experience will be valued by them?
- What is the company like? What do they do? How do they do it? What are they most proud of?

Don't forget to market yourself. Tell your future employer what they want to know. Make sure you offer the skills they are after. Remember, most of the answers will be in the job description, the graduate brochure (if there is one) and on the company website – and the company knows that too, so use them.

Fact first

Typically, half the application forms will be asking for just factual information. Our advice is to tackle the factual stuff first and get it out of the way quickly. Notes from earlier exercises and your CV will have all the information you need. Most of it you'll know anyway, such as the following:

- Name, address, telephone numbers and National Insurance number.

- Secondary and higher education – including qualifications gained.

- Employment history. Depending on the space, put in

as much as possible. They'll know you've been a full-time student so they won't be expecting the chairmanship of BP, but you can still impress them. Don't forget to mention voluntary, society and part-time work.

- Legal stuff – health, gender, race or criminal conviction disclosures (either for anti-discrimination or legal reasons). Answer honestly.

- Reference. Make sure you've asked your referees first before volunteering them. Most companies now prefer to ring, so make sure you include the phone number (and let your referees know what jobs you are applying for and give them a copy of the application form if you can).

Avoid leaving any chronological gaps – if there are any unavoidable gaps, add a credible explanation that resolves not only the gap but also the reason for the gap (for example, 'not working or at college because of viral infection, now cured and no longer a problem').

Never write 'see CV'; it's not clever, only lazy – indeed, never include your CV with an application form unless asked to do so, but don't forget to send a covering letter highlighting information on the application form as if it were a CV.

THE REST OF THE APPLICATION FORM

Regardless of how the questions are phrased, most application forms ask the same questions. The company wants to know whether you would suit the job they need to fill. So, you need to demonstrate your knowledge and interest in the job and the organisation. You need to explain why you have the skills necessary to do the job and that you're enthusiastic.

Remember, your answers should be concise. You should back up everything you say with evidence (for example, 'my work experience has fired my enthusiasm for an administration-based job, with a high element of customer interaction'). Try to vary the examples you use on your application form: it could soon become dull if every answer began with 'at band camp...'. Don't forget to use your self-branding words. And don't be afraid to draft out three or four different answers to a question – you can choose the best elements of all your answers and they'll be none the wiser.

Typical questions

Why do you want this job? Explain what attracts you to this type of work. Why does your present job make you suited to this job? Mention factors that have influenced your career choice, in particular those related to the skills you are good at and enjoy doing. If you can back up your passion for that industry by talking about any work experience, then do so. Convince them you can not only do the job, but you want to do it as well.

Give an example of when you led a team of people. What challenges did you face? This can be anything from a university project to something you did at school. The main thing is to identify the role you played in the team and how you dealt with problems that arose. If you have no experience to call on, then say so, but go on to explain how you would react in a particular situation or perhaps even talk about a team you most admire and why it is effectively managed.

Tell us about your main extracurricular activities to date. Socialising with friends is an obvious one but worth mentioning, as is your passion for films (name a couple of directors you follow), reading (name the authors or genre) and playing sport (name them). Don't forget any university societies you joined, especially if you helped organise events or held a position. Contributions to student newspapers are always good, as are unusual hobbies.

Please use this space to include any other information. An opportunity to say why you want the job, what skills you bring, to explain any glaring problems from elsewhere on the form and, of course, to say why you would like to work for that particular company or organisation.

Odd or strange questions
Some applications simply ask strange things. However, most application forms don't, but are legally vetted – an expensive and time-consuming process, which means that most companies (once they have a standard form) don't change it even if the questions aren't relevant. Regardless of how strange the questions sound, answer them – twist your answers to give them the information they want to know.

Do you have any language skills? 'Native English speaker but enthusiastic to learn a new language, therefore enrolling in an evening course in business French in the autumn.'

How would you describe yourself? Don't do any soul searching – use the information from the self-branding exercise to show them what you're made of and back it up with a couple of examples from your life: 'I am tenacious, as demonstrated by running my own magazine for two years.'

What's the most amazing experience of your life? Be passionate whatever your answer. This is an exercise of persuasion. Can you explain clearly why it was amazing? If you can show that you earned any experience through hard work or careful planning, so much the better.

Blank spaces

Never leave blank spaces – they look lazy and suspicious. Unless the form says otherwise, leave nothing blank. At the very minimum write 'not applicable', but you can turn the question to an advantage and make it work for you (for example: do have you any disabilities? 'No disabilities. I am fit and in full health due to regular swimming and squash playing').

A Quick Guide to Creating Your CV

Your CV shows employers what you've done in the past. All they know of you is what is on that sheet of paper. The impression your CV gives will determine what employers will think of you and influence their decision to ask, or not ask, you to an interview. Keep it neat, keep it well presented and keep it targeted.

We believe in a simple but effective CV (no photographs or personal statements). The examples included in this chapter are *real* CVs that got the graduates concerned interviews (and their jobs). Apart from the obvious changes to make them anonymous, they are exactly the same as when they were sent out. They are by no means 'perfect' CVs; improvements could still be made, but they are a good starting point for anybody. After all, few, if any, CVs have a 100% success rate.

Read the example CVs now (see Figures 5 and 6), before you work your way through this chapter: it will help you understand how to create your own effective CV.

RAW MATERIAL FOR YOUR CV

The following are the lists of things you will need as the raw material for your CV:

- Your qualifications and education since you were 10.
- Voluntary work, work experience and paid work.
- Your skills and achievements.
- Your hobbies and interests.

Keep these lists separate from your job-hunting research and make sure you update them regularly. If you're enthusiastic enough it's always worth creating a private 'long' CV which includes absolutely everything imaginable – it can make creating a short 'tailored' version easier.

WRITING YOUR CV

The beginning

Start with a blank page. Don't waste space writing CV or 'Curriculum Vitae' on the top of the page. Whoever reads your CV needs to know quickly who you are and how to contact you – he or she can work out it's a CV in a matter of milliseconds. Instead, you need your name and your personal details. So, include the following:

- Your name (at the very top, centred and in bold).
- Your date of birth.
- Your address (where you can be contacted for the next four months).
- Your phone number or/and mobile number and email address.

And nothing else. No one needs to know your religion, shoe size, mother's maiden name or nationality (unless you are a non-EU citizen).

Education and training

Education is probably your biggest (or only) achievement so far. If this is not the case, think carefully about perhaps putting 'employment history' before education. List your education in reverse chronological order, back until you were about 12. For each place of learning include:

- the years you were there;
- the name of the school, college or university; and
- qualifications passed.

Now you have (or are about to have) a degree, people no longer really care about your GCSEs or for that matter, your A-levels. To save valuable space, just say how many you got (i.e. '10 GCSEs') and then highlight any relevant subjects or subjects you did particularly well in (i.e. A*, A or B). Maths, English, business studies, and languages are always good to highlight. Use your judgement – if you're after a primary-school teaching position then perhaps your GCSE in physical education is worth mentioning.

A-levels only need to be listed by subject and mark – i.e. History (A), Sociology (A), English Literature (B). Put the highest grade first, followed by the others in descending order. Again, if your lowest subject is the most relevant you might want to consider putting it first in the list.

Your degree should include the overall course name and your expected, or final, degree class (i.e. 1st, 2:1, 2:2, 3rd). At this stage write a very short summary of the highlights of your degree – including any teamwork projects, extended essays or dissertations – and mention some key transferable skills. Again, relevant modules should be included (and years in industry should definitely be included).

The sneaky job-seeker can also include things in the education section that will help make his or her CV stand out as interesting. This can include education at an elite secondary schooling (Eton, etc.), or an unusual education (education abroad, especially in non-English-speaking countries). Also, mention being a school prefect or head-boy/girl.

Work experience, employment history, etc.
Again, list the most recent first followed by the rest in chronological order. This section should include work experience, work shadowing, paid work and voluntary work. Don't worry too much about the half a dozen summer or Christmas jobs you did – employers will expect you to have done them. You do not need to include them all. If you worked through an agency list it, with a short description of a type of work you did (choose the most relevant ones if possible).

The details you write depend on the job you had, and its relevance to the job you are applying for. You should include the following:

◆ The date (month and year or just year, depending on space and the aesthetic).

◆ The company or organisation (with one or two sentences, explanation of what the company does if it's not clear from the name – i.e. The British Magazine Company versus Dave Industries).

- The job title (or a short two-word job description if the job title isn't very clear).

- If relevant, your responsibilities, skills or achievements (did you do anything of note – i.e. saved the company money, established a new way of working or found a new client?).

Remember, between the work section and your education section there should be no gaps in dates. Limiting your chronology to just years helps avoid the problem of trying to match up every month although, obviously, you shouldn't lie.

Community activities and interests, or interests and other achievements

This section should always go towards the end of the CV. It is your opportunity to show yourself to be a well rounded individual who has interests other than just studying. You can also stand out from other candidates by appearing to be 'interesting'. Of course, this section can also demonstrate your other skills and self-motivation. Include the following:

- University societies – especially ones where you held a position (treasurer, etc.) or helped organise any activities (this information is voluntary, so if you're worried about the LGB or a specific political society, either don't put it in or just put 'campaign/political society).

- School and college activities – were you in the school team for any sport? Were you a prefect? Did you do any extracircular activities?

- Other community activities – do you help out at the old people's home? Do you belong to a band or a choir? Are you a member of a political party (but don't actually name it)?

- Other skills – driving licence? Computer skills? Languages? Music? Painting?

- Hobbies – don't be tempted to put just 'reading': make it interesting by putting 'passionate about reading American 1950s pulp sci-fi' or 'eighteenth-century French literature'.

- And employers love Duke of Edinburgh awards.

The end

Finish your CV with your references. It is probably best to put 'references available on request' most of the time, unless they specifically ask for them, or it makes your CV look better from a distance, i.e. there'll be a big gap otherwise.

That's it – you have the basics, now its time to polish it.

POLISHING YOUR CV

Your final CV should not be longer than two pages. Ideally, you should try to produce a one-page CV and then compare it with a two-pager. Regardless of length you should do the following:

- Keep the wording tight. Remove unnecessary words. Use simple, short sentences (for example, 'responsible for gathering information and compiling reports' compared with 'gathered information and compiled reports'.

- Use strong words: *negotiated* rather than *liaised.*

- Use the past tense.

- Avoid using I – we know it was you because it's your CV.

- Leave out poor health, reasons for leaving, trade union activity outside the NUS (unless you're applying for a TU post), place of birth and salary.

- Put in achievements (for example, that bonus for being the best sales rep in your last summer job, doubling the membership of your society within a term or any sums of money you've raised for charity).

Layout is almost as important as content:

- Make sure your CV looks balanced, with a fair amount of space.

- Use a simple font, either Arial or Times New Roman.

- Don't be afraid to leave out irrelevant or dull things in order to expand more important information or to make your CV look 'cleaner'.

- Never 'right-hand justify'; always leave the right-hand side of the page 'ragged'.

◆ Take your time. Remember, your CV demonstrates your ability to write a report and how well you can present information.

EVOLVING YOUR CV

Your CV will never be finished. There will always be new things to add, whether it's a change in jobs, a new qualification or skill, or even additional responsibilities. You should also tailor your CV to each job you apply for. However, this is not necessary for every job, especially if you're applying to a batch of jobs/companies that are very similar. But take the time to examine your CV every time you print it out to see if there are any improvements you could make. Did you leave off something last time that you should be including this time? Have you covered all the skills and experiences the employer is looking for?

Never be afraid to ask for feedback for your CV. If you do any information interviewing, don't forget to ask your contact if he or she could recommend any improvements to your CV. Of course, never be afraid to ask yourself: if I was any employer looking through a thousand CVs, why would this one stand out? How can I improve it?

A WORD OF WARNING: ELECTRONICALLY READ CVs

An increasing number of recruitment agencies and large companies are now using electronic CV readers. They are programmed to bin CVs that fail to meet the criteria (usually a preprogrammed list of 'key' words). You can rarely tell if your CV will be examined this way. So:

◆ Use key words: reflect the words used in the job ad or

description; use software names rather than generic descriptions (i.e. Excel and Lotus rather than 'spreadsheets'); and name those skills (i.e. organised, planned, executed, contributed, negotiated).

◆ Don't use any strange or unusual fonts.

◆ Don't use any underlining – use capitals or bold to emphasise.

◆ Always put dates before references (i.e. 1999–2003 university, etc.);

◆ Don't use any graphic devices.

◆ Use white A4 paper, but don't fold it or use staples.

Figures 5 and 6 are examples of CVs you may like to follow for style.

Firstname Surname

Date of Birth: 14 October 1977 Mobile: (XXXXX) XXXXXX
Address: XX Anyroad Road, City, County, XX1 1XX.
Telephone: (XXXXX) XXXXX E-Mail: name@university

Education
- 1996–99   University of East Anglia, Norwich
  Expected qualification: BA (Hons) History 2.1.
- 1994–96   Any College, Anytown, Anycounty
  GCE A-levels: English Lit. (A), History (C), Politics (D)
- 1989–94   Any School, Anytown (School Prefect)
  10 GCSEs including As in Maths and Business Studies.
- 1988–89   Island School, Hong Kong.

Work Experience
- 1999   Ad Agency Ltd: prospective work experience.
- 1998   Altered Ltd: advertising agency work experience.
  Marketed postcard service and made creative contributions.
- 1997–98   W.B.C. (beverages): managed station and led teams.
- 1997   IT tutoring: Microsoft Publisher, Excel and Access.
- 1997–97   Designed, edited and produced essay publication.
- 1995   Produced, planned and executed 30 min. film comedy.
- 1995–96   Sainsbury's: cashier.
- 1995   Shadowed Name Surname, Cambridge MP: working at Westminster, clerical work, attending meetings/functions.
- 1993–95   Established, edited and produced *WIT* magazine.

Community activities and Interests
1996–98   Uni: History Society publicity officer: created and managed campaigns. Student forum delegate.
1995–96   Co-ordinated constituency newsletter, officer, and branch chair of a local political party (Anytown).
1994–96   Committee member of 'The Information Shop', Anytown: Catalyst for 1996 Safe Sex Initiative.
1994   Duke of Edinburgh Award – Bronze.
1993–94   Oxfam 50th Anniversary Award for Community Service.

University: Member of Creative Writing and Yoga Society.
School: Active fund-raising for charity. Numerous drama productions.
Others: Attended two Arvon Foundation writing courses.

References available on request.

Fig. 5. A one page CV.

Firstname Surname

Date of Birth   24 March 1977
Email   name@university
Address   XX Anyroad Road, City, County, XX1 1XX
Telephone   (XXXXX) XXXXX

Education & Training

1996–9   University of East Anglia
BA(Hons) History: 2.1.
Final year included: dissertation and P.A.D. module (focused on transferable skills, including teamwork, presentation and report writing).

1994–6   Anytown Sixth Form College
A-levels in History (A), Sociology (A) and English Literature (B).

1990–4   Anytown High School
9 GCSEs including As in Maths, Information Technology and English, as well as Bs in French and Science.

Employment History

June/July 1999: Work placement at XYZ as a research assistant. Gathered samples, checked data and questionnaires. Responsible for delivery of internal/external mail.

March 1999: Week's work experience at QRST Ltd. Analysed transcripts from focus groups.

1998–1999: Telephone interviewer at EFGH Research. Worked on a CATI station unit. Interviewed consumers using SNAP software and paper questionnaires. Included one-day training course.

Summer 1998: Anytown Museum (voluntary work). Indexed photographs. Responsible for interviewing members of the public about making the museum and its displays more accessible to the public, included talking people through questionnaires.

Summer 1997: Receptionist: worked the switchboard and took messages.

Anytown Museum (voluntary work). Designed display, indexed photographs and artefacts.

Anytown College: secretarial assistant. Used databases and mail-merge software to write letters. Reorganised filing system.

Fig. 6. A two page CV.

Interests and other Achievements

Music
- Drummer in a band (7 years). Organised events and venues, negotiated terms, dealt with financial affairs.
- Helped develop teamwork and communication skills.
- Numerous performances, notably the Anyvillage Festival, local competitions and recording work.

Sport
- Regular squash and tennis player

University
- Committee member of University History Society: organised and planned events. Assisted publicity officer.
- Student adviser: involved personal responsibility for welfare of designated students in lower years.
- Elected fire warden of flat: responsibilities included ensuring all flat members were aware of fire procedures.
- University Tennis Society member.

College
- Form representative: organised form's events for Fun Days.
- Organised and delivered Christmas parcels for senior citizens.

School
- Prefect and form representative: attended meetings and reported back to form.
- Prizes for Service to School Sports and Effort and Progress.
- Team captain of ladies' tennis, rounders and cricket teams.

Other Skills and Qualifications
Driving   Full, clean driving licence.

Computer Skills

Good working knowledge of Microsoft Windows, Word, Excel, Powerpoint and Outlook.

Referees

Dr Personal Tutor   Further referees available on request.
School of History
Any University
Any Town
YY1 5TT
(00000) 000000

$$\left(14\right)$$

Last-minute Tips About Sending an Application

MAKING YOUR HOME YOUR PERSONAL PR DEPARTMENT (OR DISASTER)

If you share a house or flat with people (whether at university or not), make sure they know that you're job-hunting. Tell them it is important to you, and (gently) prepare them to answer the phone when you're unavailable. Make sure there is a pad and pen next to the phone (and somewhere to leave the messages). They should be told to tell anyone ringing for you that you're either in the library or perhaps just going to the shops. Under no circumstances should your flatmates be telling your future employer that you're hung-over, asleep or at the bar (or all three).

If you trust the people you live with you can also get them to become spokespeople when employers ring. It has been known for employers to vet people by using their friends. On that off-chance, make sure your flatmates understand your brand. You might also encourage them to flag up any post that arrives rather than their mysterious habit of hiding any letters under the sofa or in the fridge. And keep a folder handy by the phone with your most recent applications in it, just in case you get a surprise telephone interview at 9 a.m.

HANDWRITTEN MATERIAL

Application forms are usually best filled in by hand, and sometimes companies will ask for covering letters to be handwritten (perhaps for handwriting analysis – see Chapter 18).

Don't panic, even if your handwriting is as bad as ours. Use a pencil and a ruler (if you don't have one, buy one) to draw lines lightly across the writing area (to be rubbed out once the ink has dried) or, depending on the thickness of the paper, use a sheet of lined paper underneath as a guide. Either method will enable you to write in a straight line – the first step to writing neatly.

Use black ink (unless told otherwise) and take your time. Make sure you (and others) can read your handwriting. Remember, someone will be reading it at the other end – and if it's illegible it will be binned.

PHOTOGRAPHS

The only reason to send a picture of yourself is if you are *asked* for a photograph. The company will probably want to have a record of people they interview so that they can remember your performance, or they just want another way of sifting through applications (i.e. bin those who didn't enclose a picture). But before you jump into a photo-booth or dig out that holiday snap, stop to think about what you want your photo to say about you. One word – professionalism: you need to get a decent photograph taken. Unless it's modelling (or becoming an author) you probably won't need a professional studio shoot, but it is worth getting a decent passport photo done by a real photographer who has half-decent lighting. Machines rarely do a good enough job. In fact, let's be honest, machines make you look like an extra in a horror B-movie.

PHOTOCOPYING EVERYTHING (OR KEEPING A DRAFT)

Assuming you didn't leave everything to the last minute, photocopy any applications before you send them. Otherwise make sure you keep a draft. When you are called to an interview you need to be able to remember everything you said. After all, you're expected to be an expert on you, and interviews happen so long after writing an application you're bound to forget that really good example you used – so revise your application using your photocopy/notes.

Copies also come in useful for analysing what went wrong, should you get a negative response.

LOOKING AGAIN AT YOUR APPLICATION FORM

If you've given yourself enough time, you should be able to put your completed application on the side for a couple of days so you can come back to it afresh. It's worth taking the time to analyse your application, especially if you've had a couple days' break from job-hunting. Think about the following:

♦ What will an interviewer/employer think about you after reading the application? Will they know every-thing they need to make a fair decision?

♦ Look at any CV and covering letter from a distance, about two metres away. Does it look welcoming and easy to read? Or does it look an impenetrable block of text?

♦ Read through everything. Are there any chronological gaps?

♦ Is it targeted? Do you demonstrate your knowledge about the company? Do you show your enthusiasm for the job/industry?

♦ Don't forget spelling and grammar – don't trust that computer spell check to get anything right! Think about phrasing things more concisely. Can you improve the way you've written it?

KEEPING UP STANDARDS

No matter how many applications or letters you send, or interviews you have, always keep up your standards. It might be the hundredth or the thousandth letter you've written but, for that company, it'll only be the first time they will be receiving it, so make the effort – remember, every letter is a potential job.

ONLINE CVs AND APPLICATIONS

Online CVs and application forms are becoming more frequently used. Tackle these as you would normal application forms. Print out the instructions and any questions. Draft your answers and make sure you are happy with them before doing the real thing – use key words and your branding words.

Often you can draft in Word and 'cut and paste' on to the form which can help prevent mistakes creeping in. Check everything before clicking the Send or Finish button.

Formats vary but, typically, the online form will be broken down into skills areas, personal profiles, experiences in brief, outside activities and career objectives. None of these should present much of a problem as long as you spend time preparing and drafting. These additional sections are for the benefit of the employers who trawl through hundreds of CVs. Make sure you address the needs of each section, remembering to tailor your answers to your potential employer.

REJECTIONS . . .

Keep a list of every application you send off. Make a note when you hear anything back (from an acknowledgement to a rejection, to a come in and speak to us). Keep note of the dates. Make sure you follow up positive replies.

Don't let rejection get you down. Review the material you sent out for mistakes or reasons why they didn't ask you to interview. What can you do better next time?

NOT QUITE REJECTIONS (A NEW OPPORTUNITY)

Read your replies carefully. It's easy to dismiss any letter that doesn't say 'come in for a job' as a rejection. Keep watch for letters that say any of the following:

- Send me more details.

- Write to me in two months.

- We're keeping your CV on file.

- No vacancy at the moment, but there might be in four months.

- Would you like to come in for work experience or a temporary contract?

- We're more than happy to talk to you about the industry, although we cannot offer you...

These are all potential leads. Take them up, particularly if they are offering you temporary work (as many employers use temporary work to vet candidates). If they think there might be a vacancy in four months, write to them again in three and a half months and remind them you still exist (and are just as keen to work for them).

(15)

Well Done! Preparing for a First Interview

Congratulations! You've made it through to an interview. The time you invested in applying has paid off: they want to talk to you about your application and, more importantly, about you. Now you need to prepare for the big day. This chapter reviews the basics of the interview process from how to set up the interview to what the interview is all about (you). In Chapter 16, we examine the types of questions you may be asked. In Chapter 17 we examine what to do on the day, from what to wear to how to act. Remember, the more you prepare for an interview, the higher your chances of success.

Don't forget to treat interviews with recruitment agencies just as seriously as you would with any other employer: they need to be confident in you to uphold the agency's reputation, as well as knowing you well enough to 'sell' your services to their clients. You will need to tell an agency the area of work you are most interested in (but are willing in the short term to do any other vacancy that comes up).

SETTING UP THE INTERVIEW
When setting the date or time for the interview it should

suit both you and the company. You might, for example, prefer an interview that allows you to get a cheaper train fare. However, be flexible. Few companies will be impressed by you being unable to attend the interview within a two-week period because of your holiday commitments (educational or work commitments are a more reasonable excuse). They might even be testing your dedication by expecting you to turn up at 8.30 in the morning regardless of how far you have to travel. So if they are unwilling to budge, you can demonstrate your commitment to the job by solving the problems at your end.

Make sure you have the basics covered, if possible in writing:

◆ Get the time and day right.

◆ Know where you're going, the location of the interview (which is not always held in the main offices) and how you are going to get there (leaving plenty of time for delays and missed connections): don't forget to ask for a map or look up the address on www.multimap.co.uk.

◆ Find out who you're going to see and his or her position.

◆ Find out what position you're being interviewed for.

◆ Ask if you need to bring anything (some companies may ask you to do some 'homework' for the interview).

◆ Ask if there is any additional material they could send you to read before the interview about their company or the job (make sure you mention that it is in *addition* to your research, otherwise you're missing an opportunity to impress).

♦ Ask if there is anything you are expected to bring (certificates, portfolios, references, passport, a photograph, a presentation).

Before making your call beware that sometimes companies can play nasty tricks on candidates. Companies have been known to conduct their interviews on the phone right then and there – trying to catch you off guard. They might also indicate that they want an 'informal chat' or a 'relaxed interview' but when you turn up on the day there might be a panel of two or three interviewers. If you prepare for the worst then, no matter what they throw at you, you can come out of the ordeal their favourite candidate (or, at least, not a nervous wreck).

KNOWING WHAT TO SAY AND KNOWING WHAT THEY'RE GOING TO ASK

There are two real purposes to an interview:

1. To probe you more deeply about your suitability for the job (i.e. can you do the job?).

2. To get to know you better (i.e. are you the sort of person they want working in the company?).

3. But there is also a third purpose: you are also interviewing them. Are they the sort of company *you* want to work for?

Think of it as a PR exercise: you are trying to persuade them you are the best candidate for the job and that you are different from the other candidates. Your preparation for the interview should help you to talk in a relaxed and confident manner, although being a little nervous will help you stay focused. And your preparation will demonstrate your commitment and interest in the job and the company. Your preparation should focus on three key areas, and you should make notes for each area of anything you think is going to be important (you can then review your notes on the way to the interview).

Reviewing your written application

This will help you work out what questions they are going to ask you about *you*. So far, your written application has worked for you, and now that the company has you, in flesh and blood, they will be using your application against you. Review everything you wrote and sent them:

- Ask yourself what stands out on your CV as particularly strong or weak.

- Are there any chronological gaps?

- Is there anything that looks suspicious or strange? Perhaps you did your degree subject in the weakest of your A-level subjects, or perhaps you were captain of the cricket team in school but did no sport at university.

At this stage, you need to start thinking about the sort of questions you would want to ask yourself if you only had your CV to go by. And remember, the answers do not necessarily need to be heartbreakingly honest – they don't really want to know the deepest desires of your soul – they want to hear a good, honest explanation. Avoid whimsical answers. Remember, you might not actually remember the original reasons for doing X, but in hindsight it was a terrific decision because...

It is also tempting to try to ignore your weaknesses and omissions (in particular poor exam results or things that make you cringe). But they will ask them, so be prepared. Make sure you have an answer for every question that you would ask yourself.

Reviewing and extending your research on the company

This is the time to look back at all those notes you made previously about the company and industry you've applied to. Copy out any essential points to help refresh your knowledge on the way to the interview. Is there anything they are particularly proud of? (These notes will also help you formulate great answers to the example questions in Chapter 16).

Now is also the time to do a bit more research. Is there anything you didn't look at before? Don't forget to re-examine the job ad, job descriptions or the graduate brochure, or to check their website.

Has the company asked for any particular knowledge you should possess? What have they mentioned in the job ad, job description or in the invite to the interview? Tell them if you have this, but don't forget to refresh your knowledge with a little studying. Even if you only know the very basics, you can show you're eager to learn.

If you know anyone who works or has worked for the company, now is the time to ring him or her! Ask this person very politely if he or she knows anything about the interview process at the company:

◆ Do they have any favourite questions?

◆ Do they have any special tricks (such as deliberately interrupting interviews, or holding interviews in noisy places)?

◆ Is there anything you should avoid mentioning (such as last year's financial results or the falling share price)?

If you haven't already done so, don't forget to write a list of five questions to ask the interviewer about his or her company or the job (see Chapter 5).

Reviewing your notes on yourself and practising answering interview questions

Having done the exercises in this book to help you work out where you wanted to start your career, you can now also make use of them to answer interview questions. So, make sure you have your notes to hand and use them as you look through the next chapter on companies' favourite and most common interview questions.

KNOWING HOW INTERVIEWS WORK

Basically, an interview is where an employer asks you questions that help them decide if they want to employ you. Apart from the answers you give, there is also a certain amount of gut instinct used to make a judgement. Interviewers are, after all, only human and susceptible to the same whims that plague the rest of us.

To make the process fairer, most employers use what is called 'criteria-based interviewing'. The company draws up a list of key competencies (or criteria) to measure you against, focusing on the skills, knowledge and attitudes relevant to the job. The questions asked are scripted against the criteria and will often refer to examples of your behaviour. Your answers are then used as evidence of your abilities against the criteria for the job. The majority of the questions are not about the facts but about getting examples of the way you behaved, or how you might behave, in certain situations. For example:

♦ 'Tell me about your most difficult customer and how you dealt with them.' Or, 'How you would deal with a really difficult customer who has a complaint?'

♦ 'What has been the most important decision in your life so far, and how did you tackle it?' Or, 'What do you think will be the most important decision you'll face, and how will you tackle it?'

'Criteria-based interviewing' creates a reasonably level playing field to judge you against other candidates. Coincidentally, it also helps companies avoid accusations of racism and sexism. Criteria interviewing makes it easier to compare candidates, especially if there is more than one interviewer. Of course, there will be other criteria to meet – for example, did you arrive on time and at the correct venue? Did you dress appropriately?

There may also be some current affairs questions, particularly for financial or Civil Service jobs. For example, what do you think the Chancellor will put in his next budget? What do you think the result of a referendum on joining the euro might be? Reading a broadsheet newspaper over a few weeks before the interview should help. You don't need to know everything, just summarise the main issues and give a couple of opinions backed up by some real facts. Be prepared to argue your points, but try not to sound like a fanatic or an extremist.

(16)

Top-20 Questions

Write out your own answers to the following questions and practise them. Try to make your answers sound confident and fluent – practise with a friend or in front of a mirror if you can. Remember to think about the questions – each one can be phrased a dozen different ways. Try not to give a generic answer: the interviewer is looking for the way you respond and what makes you different from other candidates. And, it may sound obvious, but only answer the question you were asked. It is always tempting to say everything that comes into your mind. Don't.

There are two golden rules:

1. Keep your answers concise (between 30 seconds and 2 minutes), but don't give single-word answers: always explain and sell.

2. Put a positive spin on your answers: things may have gone badly but you learnt from the experience or, in the end, it worked out for the best.

Be prepared to have your answers probed a little, either for clarification or for more depth. It's really easy to dig yourself a hole if you're not prepared, and you should think before you speak (try to avoid contradicting yourself).

Questions, as you will see below, should not be taken at face value. Every question has a subtext, whether conscious or subconscious. Your answers therefore should always focus on what you can do for the employers: sell yourself and demonstrate how the company will benefit from employing you.

Keep in mind the skills you know they are looking for, by reading the job description, your research and the job ad, if there was one. Remember that you may be judged against a criterion, so make sure you use the right set of key words.

Finally, women should be extra careful. Unfortunately we don't live in an equal society (yet!). Although employers can't ask you straight out about whether you intend to have children (an expense and inconvenience for the company), there are still ways around it – beware of the subtext, especially around questions to do with flexibility, family and boyfriends/husbands.

Questions about university and your past

Few people, if any, are actually interested in what you've done. The truth of the matter is that they want to see how you went about making the decisions. Can you evaluate the outcomes of your decisions?

1. *Why did you go to X University? How did you choose X University? Why did you choose those A-levels?*

You wanted to take a course with academic stringency, and that you *acted partly on advice* from employers, teachers, careers advisers, etc. Whatever you say, never claim it was because it had a good gig scene.

Outline that you *researched* the best course: analysed the brochures, visited the university. Sell your decision – convince them it was the best choice for you.

If you went through clearing, stress why it turned out to be the best decision – what opportunities were you able to take advantage of? Was your university very strong on your degree topic? Were you able to become the head of the rowing squad (and become the catalyst for a decisive victory)?

2. Why did you do that degree? What does studying X bring to this job? What did you do on your degree?

It goes without saying that you enjoyed the topic. Perhaps you wanted to develop your strongest interest, take a new direction or conquer your weakest A-level topic. Be honest – if you did your degree despite being told you wouldn't do well, it can demonstrate resilience and tenacity. Again, mention research and a desire to do an academically rigorous subject.

Talk about your career plans and how the degree fitted in with them. Focus on those vital transferable skills. Don't bore them with too much detail about your degree – all they need is an outline of the general topics you studied. Only go into more detail if it is relevant to the job.

3. What did you like least about your last job/university? Why did you change course? What would you do differently?

Be careful not to knock everything: they do not want a whiner. A good answer would be that you didn't dislike anything in particular but if you had to single out anything it would be X. Go on to qualify it with a statement, saying that, even though you liked it less than everything else, you did it to the best of your ability and learnt something from it.

If asked about a previous employer, don't bad mouth them as your answer will reflect badly on you. If they gave you a bad reference you could maturely explain your differences and say how you would have handled the relationship differently knowing what you know now.

QUESTIONS ABOUT YOU

The interviewer wants to see preparation in your answers: clear, concise and well thought-out answers. Don't forget there will be questions about your CV and application, so make sure you know exactly what you've written.

4. *What are your strengths? What is your greatest strength? Give me five words that describe you. What sort of person are you?*

Again, resist the urge to do any soul searching. Instead, remember the word list you generated in Chapter 8 for the raw materials for your answer. Don't forget any core skills you have and what the company has said it is looking for. A good answer might demonstrate analysis, determination, the ability to get on well with others and delivering under pressure. One of the best answers we've ever been told for the five words question was 'an investment'.

Be aware that this question can also be disguised: what

words would your friends use to describe you? Again, forget what your real friends would say. Give them the same answer as if they were asking you to describe yourself, but frame it from their point of view: 'they would say I'm determined because of the time that I . . .'

5. *What are your weaknesses? What are your pet hates?*

Tailor it to the industry and the job you're after – try to work out what annoys people in your sector (i.e. crooked salespeople who ruin the industry's reputation, environmentalists who mouth off without getting their facts straight, people who don't pull their weight or people who say they can do something when they can't). Your weakness will be an intolerance of these people and your 'pet hates' are these people. Of course, it goes without saying (but therefore you should) that you would still treat them professionally and you never let them make you lose your temper.

6. *What did you not like about your last boss/tutor?*

This is a trap. A good answer would be that you don't think about these things – people are there to get on with and to get the work done. You always find that, if you act in a professional way, likes and dislikes do not really come into it. If you have a dislike make it a funny one (i.e. he always wore lime-green socks).

7. *Rate yourself on a scale of one to ten. How would your friends rate you (on the scale)?*

Assuming ten being top, we'd say eight (why would they employ anyone less?). Then justify it. This is where your branding work pays off. Remind them of your skills and your enthusiasm, which make up for anything you need to develop. Explain that you're determined to improve yourself at every opportunity.

8. *What is your favourite book? What was the last book you read? What was the last film you saw?*

It's hard not to see this as a subtle way of asking: do you read? Are you illiterate? Did you lie about reading on your CV? Equally, this question could be checking up on anything you wrote under hobbies and interests (films, theatre, role playing, visiting galleries, etc.). It is not, however, a question about personal taste unless you are applying for a cultural position. There is no harm in reading a high-brow book for appearances (Charles Dickens, for example), but the main thrust of the question is to understand you better so it's best to pick a favourite. If it's a trashy book admit it, perhaps comparing it to a less satisfying but higher-brow novel.

Whatever you choose, you need to convince the inter-viewer it was a good book and show your enthusiasm. Can you use the book to demonstrate something about you (i.e. puzzle solving, empathising with people, or being a person of action)? Whatever you choose, make sure you've read the book.

Sneaky candidates can also use this question to highlight their language skills – pick a foreign-language book that is recognisable, if possible, but not easily confused with its English translation.

9. *Give me an example of a situation where your own behaviour upset another person. Why and how did you resolve it?*

They want real examples of your abilities in action. Your answer needs to demonstrate your awareness of your impact on others. Choose a good example, preferably from a work setting. Think back to any group projects you may have done, perhaps disputes with your flatmates or a society meeting. Be clear about taking responsibility for what happened and how it was resolved; they do not want to hear you say you were totally blameless. And don't forget to tell them what you've learnt from the incident and what you would have done differently with hindsight.

10. *What are your biggest accomplishments?*

Of course, you feel your major work is ahead of you and that you have only acted in a junior position so far, but you do feel proud about X.

They want quantifiable and actual accomplishments (mention teamwork if you can). Try to add facts and figures to your example. If you were running the marathon, perhaps you beat the time you were aiming for by half an hour and came in the first 40% of finishers. If your example is about raising money for charity, tell them how much you raised and what your expectations were (and how you exceeded them).

11. *How do you handle tension? How do you cope with pressure? Tell me about your most stressful situation.*

This is not really about pressure, although you find some

pressure exhilarating and useful. It is about time management, planning ahead and not letting your nerves get the better of you. In other words, you can handle the causes of tension and stress so they do not have a detrimental effect on your work. Get bonus points, if you have a good example of where you did this, or where you learnt to do this.

QUESTIONS ABOUT THE JOB AND THE COMPANY

12. *Why do you think you will like this type of work? Do you possess the relevant skills? If not, are you willing (i.e. able) to acquire them? Why do you want this job? What skills do you bring to this job?*

This should be an easy question to answer with all the hard work you put into Chapter 3 on skills. Make sure you match up your transferable skills to those required by the employer. Cover all the prerequisite skills and *sell* any additional relevant skills. The essence of a good answer is doing your research and making sure you match as many of the company's requirements as possible.

And don't forget, you're a quick and confident learner who is eager to pick up (and improve) missing (or rusty) skills. If you can provide an example of when you learnt a new skill quickly so much the better (e.g. a crash course in Spanish for a holiday, etc.).

13. *Why this industry? Why did you apply to this organisation (Z)? What attracted you to Z? Whom else did you apply to? Why didn't you apply to X (our competitor)?*

Talk about the big picture. Obviously, you want to work for them because you feel you will be happy and do well with them. You will be able to develop your skills, be able to grow as an individual and contribute to the success of their company. Talk about what attracted you to the company; obviously, it is *not* because they are offering a job. Again, show off your research and flatter the company (e.g. it is the largest in the sector or they have a good record on environmental issues). Check their corporate literature for any interesting claims.

If you have applied to competitors it shows you are keen to get into that industry (rather than just a job). Mention your job-hunting *strategy* and demonstrate briefly that you know the differences between the organisations: why would you prefer to work with them rather than their competitors? Perhaps they are the biggest players in the market or perhaps one of the smallest; either way, back up your claims with a reason.

14. *Where do you see yourself in five years' time from now? Are you ambitious? Will you be dedicated to this company? What do you know about the structure of the industry?*

Avoid saying 'management' or something equally trite. Say instead that you want to get ahead (you are ambitious) and you'll do whatever it takes in a changing job market. Reason with the interviewer that, if you work hard and effectively, you feel rewards will follow.

If you talk about the structure of the industry, briefly mention how you know (work experience, reading, information interviewing). Talk about rising from the very bottom and say you would like to move up a realistic number of levels over time because you'll work hard and bring new skills to the job.

15. *How did you get your holiday jobs?*

Employers are looking for some strategy and planning – perhaps there were some particular skills you wanted to pick up. Employers will expect you to mention the understandable need to raise money, and you might add that you wanted to be more independently financial from your parents and had a strong desire to work during the holidays. You could even mention the job you wanted and explain why it did not happen.

If you were press ganged by your mother or your dad to get a job, turn it to your advantage (i.e. it gave you the taste for hard work, taught you what you didn't want to do or, if it's the same industry, it got your passions burning).

16. *Which jobs did you like least? Do you like routine tasks/ regular hours?*

Never say you were bored in your last job – after all, every employer wants you to do some amount of menial or administrative work. Pick on the most boring job. It taught you lessons in 'sticking to it' and helped you know yourself better, but you would rather have had one that stretched you more.

Of course, most graduates hate routine and would love a stimulating job. However, routine is mainly where it is at.

So tell them, of course stimulating work is what everyone wants, but you realise from part-time work/writing essays that routine work is very important and has to be done. You have always approached it willingly and energetically.

17. *Are you flexible and mobile? We're a fast-growing company. Does that cause you any problems?*

Damned if you do. Damned if you don't. Ask for clarification: what do they mean? Is it travel on business or relocation of the company? Is it long hours or flexible shifts? A 'no' usually means your chances are blown; companies want slaves. What they want to hear is that you have no ties and you'll walk on burning coals for them.

Be honest: you don't just want a job but a career, so you've accepted the fact that you will have to make some sacrifices, and you're prepared for a certain amount of travel/overtime.

18. *How long will it take you to make a contribution to this company? What can you offer this organisation that others can not?*

Say it will take a few weeks to settle down. However, you pride yourself on being a quick learner and having loads of 'get up and go'. You could follow up by asking what their entry training plan is for graduates (if they have one!). Remember, they don't really care at this stage how much you know, but how much you care (i.e. how much you are willing to give the company).

SCENARIO AND BEHAVIOURAL QUESTIONS

19. *Give me an example of a time when you had to work as part of a team. What has been the biggest obstacle you've had to overcome? Tell me of a time when you had to give bad news to someone? Tell me how you would deal with the situation . . .*

These questions will vary depending on the types of things they are after – for example, teamwork, self-confidence/ tenacity, drive and initiative, tolerance to pressure, information gathering or analytical skills. Regardless of what they're after, you'll need to explain what happened, how you reacted, how you might have reacted differently with hindsight and what the outcome was. You should take responsibility for the outcome. It might have ended in disaster so you could say, for example, 'I made a mistake that time by not trusting other members of the group' or 'I wasn't as experienced in time management then as I am now . . .'.

Of course, if you haven't had any experience of a particular scenario then you should pick a similar experience and tell the interviewer 'nothing exactly like that has happened to me, but there was this one occasion . . .', etc.

HOSTILE QUESTIONS

Interviewers like to try to push you over the edge a little, especially if you've said you cope with hostility and pressure easily. However, with a little thought, even the most hostile question can be turned around in your favour. Remember, at the end of the day it's your answer that counts, not the question they asked, so don't lose your temper or get too defensive.

Don't forget, if anyone throws you a question that's a real toughie, you can buy time with little phrases, such as 'That's a tough question, now let me see. I would have to answer...' and 'I'm glad you asked me that question...'.

And there is nothing wrong with just asking for a moment to consider the answers. Even halfway through giving an answer you can ask for clarification (for example, 'Is this the type of answer you are looking for?').

20. *Surely your degree has nothing to do with this job?*

True, on the surface your degree might appear to have nothing to do with this job, but the transferable skills you started to develop doing your degree will benefit the company. Then give an example.

(17)

On the Day of the First Interview

You've done your preparation – reviewed your notes, thought of answers to potential questions and you've got your own questions to ask the interviewer. Now it's time to make sure you look the part and to familiarise yourself with the process so you're ready for whatever they throw at you.

PAYING ATTENTION TO YOUR IMAGE

No matter how well you shine in an interview, if you let yourself down by your appearance you've blown it. First impressions count, and you will be judged by your appearance (i.e. what you wear and what you don't wear). This is not about ethics or fairness; it's human nature to judge other people by first impressions – i.e. what we see with our eyes. Use it to your advantage; make sure that the judgement is made in your favour. If you take time and effort over your appearance, it shows you are taking the interview seriously; in the eyes of the interviewer you become a serious candidate, a real option!

Wear a suit to all your interviews. If you don't have a suit and can't afford one, look in your local charity shops (Oxfam, etc.) for one. Few employers will expect you to wear a brand-new Armani suit. They just want to see you make an effort. Make sure you wear a freshly ironed shirt or blouse, clean clothes and polished shoes. Don't dress sexually provocatively as not only does this give a bad impression but it can also make the interviewer feel uncomfortable (especially if he or she doesn't know where to look!). If you think a suit might be overdoing it, fine, but always err on the side of smarter than expected.

PERSONAL APPEARANCE CHECKLIST

✓ Pay attention to the 'tops and toes'. Make sure your hair has been cut recently and that your shoes are polished.

✓ Get your hair cut the week before. It should look professional and you should feel comfortable with it. Men shouldn't shave their head (unless they're balding) as it looks aggressive.

✓ Glasses and contact lens – always wear glasses (if you have the choice *and feel comfortable*) as they tend to make people look more intelligent and mature.

✓Go easy on any make-up – too much gives the impression of insecurity, poor judgement or something to hide. Don't worry about any spots, everyone gets them. What is more important is how you 'carry yourself off' (i.e. how you behave).

✓ For men – earrings are out but quality ties are in (as an advertising creative director once said, ties are the only jewellery a man should wear; always choose an expensive tie over a handful of cheap ones).

✓ For women – choose your accessories carefully: avoid any big or oversized jewellery.

✓ Personal hygiene – always brush, floss and use a mouthwash. Don't drink any coffee or tea or eat anything that smells (garlic, spicy food, etc.) before the interview (indulge your taste buds afterwards).

✓ Wash thoroughly – use an anti-dandruff shampoo if you're so afflicted, and make sure your nails are clean (attention to detail!).

✓ If your normal deodorant usually lets you down, use a sports deodorant with an anti-perspirant but avoid excessive perfume.

✓ Facial hair counts against men, as politicians have known for years. Go clean shaven; you can have a beard when you get the job.

✓ Hide any tattoos and remove any other body adornments (nose, eyebrow, tongue studs, etc.). This stops people jumping to conclusions about the type of person you are. Once they know you they'll be more accepting of your personal eccentricities.

✓ Check your eyes for 'sleep' – a small thing that could easily destroy that carefully cultivated image of a dynamic self-starter.

✓ If in doubt about interview dress code, phone and ask. It shows initiative.

PACKING A SURVIVAL KIT

Pack a small survival kit for the journey to your interview. Use a compact, professional-looking bag (preferably black).

A SURVIVAL KIT CHECKLIST

✓ A card with your questions on it (kept somewhere easy to find).

✓ A map of where you are going and details of where the interview is.

✓ Three freshly printed copies of your CV (updated since your application).

✓ Pen and paper.

✓ A calculator for any potential aptitude tests.

✓ Your notes about the company to read before arriving, as well as a copy of everything you sent in your application.

✓ Any evidence you might need (particularly important for creative industries such as journalism and design work).

✓ A watch – and arrive no more than ten minutes early. Make sure the watch won't bleep during the interview.

✓ Sticky plasters (for blisters).

✓ Painkillers and a small bottle of water (for headaches).

✓ A spare pair of tights (if wearing a pair).

✓ Imodium or other anti-diarrhoea tables (for nerves).

✓ A couple of safety pins (for when trousers/skirt fastenings break).

✓ A needle and thread (for when buttons unexpectedly fall off).

✓ Hair brush/comb (for a wind-swept tidy-up).

✓ Money (for cab fares, train fares, etc.).

✓ Nail-file (for broken fingernails).

✓ A mobile and the company's telephone number to use immediately if there is any chance you are going to be late. Turn off your mobile phone before entering the building of your potential employers. If you forget, don't answer it if it rings, just apologise and turn it off! Remember to be professional.

✓ A chocolate bar to keep your blood-sugar level up.

✓ Your smile.

ARRIVING FOR THE INTERVIEW

Bear the following points in mind when you arrive for the interview:

◆ Arrive on time (no more than ten minutes prior to the interview time).

◆ Introduce yourself with a firm handshake and a smile (if you're not used to introducing yourself or shaking hands, practise).

◆ If you have a cold/flu, apologise at the start of the interview. Have fresh tissues ready and don't cough or sneeze without using a tissue (not only is it unhygienic and unpleasant but you also risk giving the interviewer your cold).

◆ Not accepting any drinks is usually the best way to avoid spilling any on yourself or needing to go to the loo halfway through the interview. Choose water if you are tempted.

PROFESSIONAL BEHAVIOUR

Be polite to everyone. You probably won't know the managing director from the cleaner, so make sure you treat everyone with respect. Often receptionists and secretaries are also asked to evaluate candidates secretly, so abuse them at your peril!

It's worth being on your best behaviour from the moment you leave your house. You never know until it's too late if your interviewer was sitting opposite you on the train (sounds unlikely, but it can happen!). And don't smoke, either at the interview or anywhere near the interview location.

LISTENING CAREFULLY TO QUESTIONS

Make sure you understand the question. If you don't, ask for clarification. What did you mean by X? Did you want me to talk about Y? You can also use this as a technique to buy extra time for questions that have stumped you. Occasionally, you may even ask for a moment or two to think about the answer. As long as you don't do it for every question, it may even help you come across as intelligent and a thinker.

And be yourself – modifying any extreme behaviour you might have, of course! Don't forget your personal branding (use your self-branding key words when talking about yourself). And remember to act as you speak: don't claim 'attention to detail' if you can't remember the interviewer's name.

ENGAGING WITH THE INTERVIEWER

Share the conversation; you should both be talking in

equal amounts. Remember, the interviewer wants to find out more about you, so make sure your answers are longer than a couple words. Besides, every question is an opportunity to sell yourself as the best candidate for the job – don't lose that chance. If you're not sure about your answer, ask: is this the answer you were looking for? Would you like me to explain further?

Be kind to your interviewer. He or she will be just as nervous as you. If you can get the interviewer to relax and enjoy the interview, he or she will thank you. Your interviewer probably isn't a clever and manipulative psychologist. He or she might not even be trained to do interviews. Try to help by adding energy and enthusiasm, but don't talk over the interviewer or interrupt mid-sentence, no matter how boring the interviewer is. And don't forget, the pressure is on the interviewer: will he or she recommend the right candidate? Will he or she choose the wrong candidate? Will you make a fool of the interviewer if you were hired?

Do not panic if there is a lull in the conversation. You might be tempted to say anything just to fill the void. Don't. The interviewer might just be collecting his or her thoughts. If the silence lasts more than a minute, ask the interviewer if he or she has any further questions, or if you should expand on a particular subject. There is also an opportunity to suggest items from your own agenda for conversation.

WATCHING YOUR BODY LANGUAGE
Don't fidget or look bored. Make sure you show you are

interested/paying attention (nod, make eye contact, etc.). Be careful not to cross your arms. Try not to play with anything in your pockets or to fiddle with anything else, such as your hair, loose change or watch strap. Smile occasionally and stay relaxed. Remember, you're also sizing them up as well: do you want to work for them? And don't forget the interviewer's body language. Keep an eye out for any signs that your answers are too long or too short or that you've misunderstood a question.

SNEAKY INTERVIEW TECHNIQUES

You can never tell if an interview is going to be deliberately interrupted or held in a noisy environment. Genuine mistake or not, it can reveal much about how you handle yourself and react. Just try to take everything in your stride. Nothing is worth getting upset or angry about and, if you act calm and solve any problems that do arise, you can only get extra credit.

Sometimes the other candidate who is sitting next to you in reception isn't what he or she seems. He or she might just be last year's graduate sent to spy on you and take 'informal' notes, so be careful what you say!

And, don't be fooled by anyone who is over-friendly or hostile. This may be a ploy to get you to reveal *the real you*. Remember, the interview is an unnatural environment; you are being tested the whole time – treat it as such.

AT THE END

Don't forget to ask *your* questions at the interview. You

might want to ask about training and how they plan to develop you as a graduate. Never ask about salary or benefits; wait until they offer you the job. Don't forget those impressive questions that were generated by your research (see Chapter 4 for a reminder).

If you are asked how you thought the interview went, always try to leave on a positive note: it went really well or not as badly as you thought it would and that you're looking forward to working for the company.

Thank the interviewer for his or her time and ask when you should expect to hear from the company. They should (although not always) contact you and let you know whether or not you have the job, or if they would like you to come back for a second interview or attend an assessment centre.

SEXIST AND RACIST INTERVIEWERS

Companies that allow people who are sexist or racist to conduct interviews are opening the door to expensive lawsuits. You do not have to put up with any form of harassment while applying for or doing a job. Take pride in yourself – if this is how they treat potential employees, do you really want to work for them? If you experience any such incident you should contact:

- the Equal Opportunities Commission (www.eoc.org.uk);
- the Commission for Racial Equality (www.cre.gov.uk);
- or, for physical assaults, the police.

Whatever is said during the interview, you should remain calm. Tell the interviewer you are offended by his or her overt sexual or racial comments. Ask to speak to his or her superior, or leave straightaway, but don't lose your temper. As soon as you are safely away from the building write down everything that happened (as difficult as it may be at the time) word for word and contact the appropriate organisation. Remember, you have done nothing wrong; it is the person who was abusing you who has probably broken the law and endangered his or her job. You should also write to the head of human resources, or the managing director, to explain why you left the interview. If you do not hear from the company, then you are well shot of that organisation.

AFTERWARDS

A quick post-interview analysis
Find somewhere quiet where you can sit down for half an hour to conduct a post-interview analysis. Jot down any notes that might help you in your next interview:

◆ Did any of the questions catch you off guard? Did you make any mistakes?

◆ What were your best answers? What got a good response from the interviewer?

◆ If you had to repeat it all again, what would you do again? What wouldn't you do again?

Failing to get the job
First, don't let it get you down. You did well getting an interview – remember, each interview is a step closer to getting that job.

Second, most companies are more than willing to offer feedback about your interview performance and reasons why you didn't get the job. It feels a little strange asking for the feedback but worth it. Their advice might help you in your next interview and get you your dream job! Remember to ask politely and not to argue with your feedback. It's a chance for you to learn something about yourself, not to convince them they made the wrong decision. If you were asked to complete any tests (see Chapter 18), you should ask for feedback on them as well.

Finally, as soon as they say 'no' to you, you can ask them if they know anyone else who is hiring. Ask them for any advice they might be able to give on how to crack that industry. You never know, they might have a gem or two for you.

Dealing with Second Interviews

WHY ONE INTERVIEW WASN'T ENOUGH

Congratulate yourself on being asked back. They like you and want to get to know you better. Most likely, they have a short list of candidates (from two to twenty is the normal range) and want to make the best selection humanly possible from that list. They are, after all, planning to spend money on employing, training and rewarding you. Whatever you do, don't be disheartened and don't drop out. Remember, each round is a step closer to getting that job.

COPING WITH THE NEW DANGERS

The employer has got a good impression of you. They now want to interrogate you and your skills further. Nothing mentioned in this chapter is restricted to second-round interviews. Some companies may use these selection aids before the first interview or perhaps during a third round, if at all. When you are asked to attend any additional interviews you should be told a general outline of what will happen; if not, ask. Many employers use assessment centres as part of their second-round process, in which case you might be asked to attend one or two days of exhausting, but exhilarating, work, including tests, group exercises and social occasions.

While none of this comes cheap for the company (the final bill will run into thousands of pounds), the results are not taken in isolation. The impression you give will still count, so try to remain enthusiastic and upbeat no matter what they throw at you.

GROUP PROJECTS AND TEAM EXERCISES

What better way to assess a 'group player' than in a group situation? You will be put into a group with other candidates (although can you be sure they are all genuine?) and your group will be given a specific task to complete (from building a tower out of paper and sticky tape to designing and selling a product). Exercises range from the silly to the ultra-serious. Whatever the task is, take it seriously – this is about assessing your group skills in order to give you that dream job. Remember, the final outcome doesn't matter as much as how you get there (i.e. together).

If someone is appointed leader by the assessors, he or she is the group leader. Do not get involved in group power struggles or become the group dictator. The assessors are looking for real team players, not the people who say and do nothing or those who say the most and do everything.

The safest policy is to play the role of a facilitator. Help guide the group gently. Encourage everyone to get along with each other (as you would in the real world and if this was your team). Keep the group focused by occasionally summarising what has been decided and by reminding people when the group has forgotten what they agreed.

Use your body language to show you're listening. Don't forget the assessors will be watching your verbal communication skills as well. While you'll want to convince others by using reason and logic, you must be open to being convinced yourself. The assessors may be looking for people who can be convinced by a sound argument or who are willing to go enthusiastically with the group consensus (a real team player). No matter what happens you should stay calm, relaxed, have fun and get stuck in.

PSYCHOMETRIC TESTING

Psychometric tests are designed to measure your mind and your attitudes. Nearly all these tests (sometimes called personality inventories) measure your preferences for things – for example, if you prefer to avoid conflict or to address issues immediately.

These tests are not generally used for selection purposes but they are designed to help understand you better. Sometimes employers will discuss these results with you, either as a starting point to a discussion on how you act in certain situations or, for larger employers, how they might train you and what areas they would recommend you work in.

The good news is that there are no right or wrong answers and you'll be given a reasonable, if not generous, amount of time to fill in the test. Pay close attention to any instructions you are given and answer the questions honestly. (For aptitude tests, see Chapter 19.)

GRAPHOLOGY AND ASTROLOGY

It has been known. Graphologists look at handwriting and astrologists read your horoscope. You don't do much, except provide a handwriting sample (choose carefully!) and your birth date. If asked what you think – remember if your employer uses it, then they probably believe in it. Besides, if it works in your favour, why should you care? After all, you were the ideal candidate anyway because...

PREPARING A FIVE-MINUTE PRESENTATION

A favourite request of interviewers, no matter how long you've been working or what course you did, is to give you half an hour to prepare a five-minute presentation. The art of a succinct and interesting presentation is a difficult one, so it's worth having one up your sleeve just in case.

Keep it simple. Some of the best presentations have been on making a cup of tea or replacing a light bulb. If you have a choice of what you're going to talk about, make sure it's something you know well. Avoid sensitive or moral issues. Make notes of what you're going to say. Structure your talk carefully – tell them what you're going to say, say it and then remind them what you've told them. Don't overload them with information. You want them to be able to remember what you've told them. Any strange or interesting nuggets of fact always go down well and keep audiences listening.

Once you're up, forget the audience – size doesn't matter. You're not talking to ten people but ten people individually. It should feel no different from talking to just one person – you need to speak clearly and make sure everyone is following what you're saying. Maintain eye contact and watch your body language. Feel confident: they want to hear what you've got to say and, more importantly, how you say it.

OTHER SOLO EXERCISES

There is almost no limit to what an employer might ask you to do to demonstrate your abilities. Chefs often ask candidates to fry an egg or bake a soufflé to demonstrate their cooking skills. Think about the post you're applying for and the sort of things you might be expected to do. Try to find some way of practising beforehand. For example, advertising companies love client services candidates to role-play 'selling' ads to clients, which can be practised by trying to 'sell' an ad from a newspaper to a friend.

You might be asked to write a report based on a pile of information. Just remember that, with reports, conciseness is the key. You want to summarise any key findings, taking the very essence out of the information. Don't forget to ask if there is a preferred length or style to the report and who the target audience is intended to be. It'll help you and look impressive.

The 'In-tray' exercise is still used, although some companies are updating it by using an email simulator. You need to demonstrate how you handle complex information and how you make priorities. Some things may be urgent but deeply unimportant. Always do the tasks that are most important and most urgent first, and the least urgent last. Part of this process might also be drafting replies to letters – an ideal chance to demonstrate your brilliant written communication skills.

UNUSUAL LOCATIONS AND SITUATIONS

Lunch/dinner. Second interviews/assessment centres, especially held over a day or two days, usually have an opportunity to attend a lunch or dinner with the other candidates and staff from the company. Go, even if it's 'optional'.

Whatever they say about being off the record, do not be lulled into a false sense of security. It is still part of the interview process. Avoid ordering the most expensive item on the menu and don't get drunk.

Pubs. Sometimes you might be invited to an interview/ chat over a drink. Remember, it is still an interview/ business meeting despite the relaxed atmosphere and whatever the company said. You always enjoyed the assessment day/interview, although you found it challenging. Be prepared to drink and relax, but do so in *moderation*. You will already be high on adrenaline and you don't want to confess anything you would not have otherwise said during an interview.

Noisy locations. Never let it throw you: it's a test of your ability to keep calm under unusual circumstances.

Interruptions. Another test to measure your reactions. Are you the sort of person who gets upset when interrupted? Someone who will be easily angered by co-workers and clients?

Panel interviews. Panels are usually two to four people, although there could be more (and it is scary being interviewed by eight people). The best thing to do is remain calm and give your answers to the person who asked the question, but not forgetting to give the rest of the panel an occasional glance and smile.

(19)

Preparing for an Aptitude Test

Aptitude tests, unlike psychometric tests, examine your abilities and skills, particularly IQ (intelligence), literacy (verbal reasoning) and numeracy (maths). There are right and wrong answers and the results will probably be used to help make a selection for the job – usually in association with an interview. These tests are sometimes also used to help identify areas of weakness for staff development and to place personnel appropriately within an organisation. So, your goal must be to get the best results you can (so that you're close to, equal to or better than the nearest competition).

The good news – practising ability tests will increase your scores. Practising will not improve your skills but will improve your ability to answer the questions, just like warming up before a race helps athletes go that little bit faster. Try the two sample tests in this chapter (the answers are in Appendix D) as a start, but also think about the following:

◆ Doing crosswords, and other word-based puzzles.

◆ Doing maths without using a calculator – try adding up the money you spend during a week in your head or adding up your bank statement.

- Find more example tests – look in your careers centre, local library or bookshop for one of the hundred books on the subject.

Remember, when you sit any aptitude test:

- Pay careful attention to any instructions you receive.

- Stay calm, relaxed and focused.

- There will be a time limit, so if you can't answer a question skip it.

- The questions will get harder as the test goes on – so don't worry, just try your best to answer as many as possible.

- The tests are usually designed never to be finished in the time allowed – so there is a fine balance between speed and accuracy.

- Bring your own calculator and don't use the calculator function on a mobile phone – not only could it ring during the test (which is part of the interview) but you could also be accused of cheating via text messaging.

- Don't forget to get a good night's sleep the day before.

PRACTICE TEST 1

You have seven minutes to complete this test. You can use a calculator.

Verbal questions

Choose the combination of words that makes the most sense:

1. The _____ of the campaign will be _____ by the direct response created by the campaign and by the number of units sold.

   a) successes, measure
   b) successfulness, calculate
   c) success, measured
   d) failure, determined
   e) succeed, indicated

2. The company is _____ to keeping _____ satisfaction at a high level. As a result, we are giving everyone a bonus this year.

   a) committed, employer
   b) intent, employed
   c) devoted, employment
   d) committed, employee
   e) apathetic, employee

3. Her first step in _____ her presentation was to _____ the topic she was to talk about.

   a) writing, define
   b) creating, defy

c) delegating, ignore
d) sharing, doubt
e) closing, widen

4. It is the company's main aim to keep any admin and extra paperwork _____ by these new regulations to a _____. If you are over-burdened please talk to your line manager.

a) created, maximum
b) reduced, minimum
c) created, limit
d) generated, minimum
e) generalised, maximum

Numerical questions

Choose the correct answer from the five options given:

1. Temporary staff are paid £4.50 per hour. If 37 hours were worked last week by each of seven temporary staff, what was the total bill?

a) £397
b) £582
c) £845.5
d) £1,165.5
e) £1,974

2. A survey carried out on 2,500 people showed that 47% liked a new product while 17% were indifferent. If the rest said they disliked the product how many people were in this category?

a) 36

b) 637

c) 900

d) 945

e) 1120

3. In an average week a vital piece of machinery is not in operation for 1.25 hours. Lost revenue per hour is £648,000. What is the approximate total revenue lost in a 52-week year?

a) £0.8m

b) £8.04m

c) £12.10m

d) £42.1m

e) £142m

Numerical analysis questions

Choose the correct option using the data:

Staff profile

Function		Length of service in years	
Administration	44%	0–5	16%
Production	56%	6–15	28%
Total staff	275	16–25	24%
		26–35	24%
		36+	8%

1. How many more production staff are there than administrative staff?

a) 12

b) 27

c) 33

d) 110

e) Cannot Say

2. How many administrative staff have served
   between 10 and 20 years?

   a) 31
   b) 57
   c) 72
   d) 89
   e) Cannot say

3. How many of the administrative staff are there in
   the 26–35 years' service group if the proportion of
   production staff and administrative staff is the
   same for this group as for the overall group?

   a) 11
   b) 29
   c) 37
   d) 49
   e) 52

4. If half the 0–5 years service group and all the 36+
   years service group are production staff, how
   many production staff are there altogether in the
   other groups?

   a) 110
   b) 132
   c) 164
   d) 231
   e) Cannot say

PRACTICE TEST 2

You have eight minutes to complete this test. You can use a calculator.

Verbal test

There are two passages below. Each passage is followed by three statements. Evaluate each statement based on the information or opinions contained within the relevant passage. Select your answer according to the rules given below.

Mark **A** if the statement is true or follows logically, given the information or opinions contained in the passage.

Mark **B** if the statement is untrue or the opposite follows logically, given the information or opinions contained in the passage.

Mark **C** if you cannot say without further information.

Passage 1

The rules that govern acceptable advertising practice are a combination of codes of conduct and legal obligations that all advertising must adhere to. Commonsense and public opinion also play an important role. However, many companies and agencies take into account more practical considerations when deciding to run an advertisement, particularly if intending to utilise the advertising concept for a short duration only, risking punishment if the reward of public awareness is worth it.

1. Advertisers are under legal obligations for which they risk punishment if they disregard them.
   A   B   C

2. Advertising is always acceptable if it adheres to both codes of conduct and legal restrictions.
   A   B   C

3. Companies take into account practical considera-
    tions when deciding to disregard advertising
    rules. A   B   C

Passage 2
In the name of both profit and low environmental impact, on
many long haul flights, aircraft fly at high altitudes, at around
33,000 feet or above. This means an aircraft will consume less
fuel than if it was flying at 30,000 feet, therefore releasing less
CO_2, also known as greenhouse gas. However, by flying higher
the aircraft produces contrails, which are linear ice trails that
can linger in the sky for hours. These contrails contribute more
to the effects of global warming, by trapping heat, than the
additional fuel consumed by flying lower.

1. Aircrafts should flyer higher, at 33,000 feet or
    above, to minimise their effect on global warming.
    A   B   C

2. The linear ice trails called contrails are formed by
    aircraft flying at 33,000 feet or above. A   B   C

3. Smaller aircraft produce less CO_2 than larger
    aircraft. A   B   C

Numerical test

Years	Index of unit value of industrial production USA
1929–1930	106
1930–1931	89
1931–1932	67
1932–1933	78
1933–1934	85
1934–1935	102
1935–1936	120
1936–1937	128
1937–1938	100
1938–1939	127

1. What percentage of industrial production was achieved in 1932–1933 when compared to 1929–1930?

   a) 112%
   b) 74%
   c) 126%
   d) 60%
   e) 70%

2. What percentage of industrial production was achieved in 1929–1930 when compared to 1932–1933?

   a) 26%
   b) 36%
   c) 74%
   d) 136%
   e) 160%

3. By how many percent was 1938–1939 production above 1931–1932?

   a) 0.89%
   b) 89%
   c) 1.87%
   d) 187%
   e) 18.7%

Year	Average monthly unemployment (000s)	Net annual Immigration
1955	213.2	27,550
1956	229.6	800
1957	294.5	23,020
1958	410.1	15,020
1959	444.5	16,390
1960	345.8	49,670
1961	312.1	66,290
1962	431.9	35,051
1963	520.6	7,928
1964	372.2	14,848
1965	317.0	13,400
1966	330.9	9,620
1967	521.0	10,080
1968	549.5	4,801
1969	543.8	688
1970	582.2	1,749
1971	758.4	−1,163
1972	844.1	1,176
1973	597.9	−2,130
1974	599.7	5,845

4. What was the average unemployment rate in the years 1961–1966?

    a) 280,000
    b) 308,000
    c) 318,000
    d) 381,000
    e) 508,000

5. What was the total immigration figure from 1969 to 1974?

    a) 16,065
    b) 6,165
    c) 616

    d) −616

    e) −6160

6. What is the answer if you divide the figure obtained in question 5 into the unemployment number for 1958?

    a) .6652

    b) 6.652

    c) 66.52

    d) 665.2

    e) 6652

(20)

Prozac for Job Hunters

We want (and expect) you to get your dream job in the shortest time possible, but you need to be prepared for the process to take some time. One of the biggest reasons people don't end up in their dream career is that they give up. So, if you're prepared for the six months or longer job hunt, you have a better chance of getting that perfect job.

The secret to your success will be how you manage your own motivation. Yes, it can be hard to continue in the face of almost constant rejection, but don't just quit your hunt and plump for any old job that comes along – work by all means, but if it isn't your ideal job, keep searching.

The simplest way to feel positive about you search is to remind yourself how much effort you have already put in. From now on, keep a record of every moment you spend job-hunting (including reading this book). It doesn't have to be elaborate. Make a note of the time you spend researching, writing letters, filling out applications, preparing for interviews and being interviewed. This will help you visualise your progress. You can also use the list to keep check on yourself. There can be no pretending to have done a busy week job-hunting with the truth written in ink.

Try setting yourself firm goals. For example, send out twenty speculative letters this week or spend three hours a day researching new potential contacts. Whenever you meet or exceed any of your goals, reward yourself – do something that you'll enjoy (e.g. go out for the evening or watch your favourite movie).

The support of friends and family can also be an invaluable tool in banishing those job-hunting blues, but be careful that these friendly faces don't do more harm than good. Filter their sympathy through your 'bullshit antenna', watching out for the advice and pressure to take jobs that are clearly wrong for you.

Never be afraid to take a well earned break. Sometimes, when you're at your most relaxed, inspiration can strike: a new way to write that covering letter, a new list of employers to tackle or, even, a new approach to the whole thing.

NOT TAKING REJECTION PERSONALLY

Don't fear rejection: it's just part of the process. If you start letting the fear of rejection influence you, you'll soon stop applying for jobs. Being rejected by an employer doesn't say anything about you as an individual. Sometimes employers will reject applications for the strangest of reasons, mostly just to get the pile of CVs down to a manageable level. Just remember that, in five years' time when you've been doing your dream job for however long, every rejection was just a step closer to finding that perfect job.

Persistence gets the job, not self-pity.

Be aware that you need to keep up your self-esteem. If your confidence is beginning to slide take action immediately. Remember, there are plenty of jobs out there, but you want the right job. Remind yourself of your goal: the career you have set out to achieve.

While you're waiting, keep building your CV. There is plenty of part-time and temporary work out there, particularly through agencies. And there are thousands of organisations desperate for volunteers. These 'stop-gap' jobs can be great for your mental and, sometimes, even your financial health. Be conscious, however, that you will have to resist the temptation of giving up your job hunt. Consider it very carefully if you do: it may be that you've stumbled on a brilliant career path you hadn't even known existed, or it might just be those voices of doubt steering you off course.

The post-interview rejection can feel worse than the post-application rejection. They've actually met you but still didn't want you for that job. Don't take it personally. Try to be positive: you had a real interview! They're an invaluable experience. Remember, every interview you go to is (you've guessed it) a step closer to that dream job.

We've said it before – ask for feedback. Most companies these days will gladly give ten minutes of constructive feedback to candidates who have been interviewed. And, don't be afraid to ask for it. They've already said they don't want to offer you a job, they can't do anything worse. But, whatever you do, don't argue with their feedback, just listen. They may offer you a gem or two of advice, which could make the next interview a winner.

Avoid setting all your hopes on a single interview or application. We've all been there, praying for that single event to deliver all our dreams. Don't. It's bound to disappoint if you do. As soon as the interview is over and you've made notes on your performance, give yourself a pat on the back and start preparing for the next opportunity/interview.

FINAL GEMS OF WISDOM

First, don't be afraid to change. There is always a better way to communicate something more effectively. And there will always be something you forgot to mention in your CV, from that coveted Duke of Edinburgh award to that year when you were treasurer of the Music Society. Review everything. Look out for your mistakes. We all make them, but many of us never learn from them. Those who do can achieve greatness.

Secondly, always be persistent. Never give up.

Thirdly, don't be afraid to change your strategy. Sometimes, especially after several months of unsuccessful hunting, a fresh start is the best way to continue. It can bring renewed vigour to your campaign. There are plenty of websites, books and newspaper articles out there that recommend different courses of action. Consider each one carefully if you're going to change methods: does it work at all? Will it work for you?

Fourthly and finally, don't apply for jobs you don't want. It's a waste of energy and time. Instead, focus on different routes to the job you do want (remember that cunning plan? It's time to look at the other options). And don't forget it is okay to take a 'stop-gap' job to keep money coming in and keep your CV chronologically complete, but be firm with yourself about what you're doing and why. Write down the maximum time you are going to do that stop-gap job and what you're going to do in the meantime to further your career ambitions (i.e. 'I am not going to do this job for more than six months and I will spend twelve hours every week looking on job websites for the job I really want and writing speculatively to ten new companies every week').

Part three

Beyond your first job

(21)

Planning for Your Next Job or Career

Congratulations: you've started work and you're well on your way to your dream career. You've looked through Appendix C for our tips for getting ahead in the world of work. You might think there is nothing left but to get on with the job you've been employed to do. However, there is plenty you can do to:

- enhance your career progress (preparation for promotion);

- insulate yourself against redundancy;

- be ready for any new opportunities (for example, when head-hunters come calling or you bump into the boss of a rival firm and strike up a good relationship); and

- get ready for your next career, whatever it may be.

STEP 1: KEEPING YOUR CV UPDATED
Your CV has been an effective weapon in getting you to where you are now. Don't let time blunt it. Every time you do something *new* or achieve something, add it to the long version of your CV, so you have an up-to-date resource to help you compile a fresh CV. With a computer (or even by hand) it only takes a matter of minutes to make a note of your new responsibility or achievement.

Keeping a note of your achievements and responsibilities is also invaluable for any appraisals you have (and you should have one once a year). No one else will keep a score of your success but someone is bound to keep a score of your failures. Make sure you have enough ammo to fight them.

STEP 2: FEEDING YOUR NETWORK

Hopefully, your network has played an important role (directly or indirectly) in helping you get your job. Like your trusty CV, now is *not* the time to let your network wither and die but a time to nurture it and help it grow. Write letters or speak to key people in your network to let them know how you're doing – thank them for any help they gave you. Try to keep the dialogue going between you and each member of your network. And keep adding new people.

Don't forget to help people below you to rise. Most universities run (via the careers centre) a 'contact in industry scheme'. UEA operates one called 'Careerlink', giving students the opportunity to speak to people who have careers the students want to pursue. It, of course, doesn't just benefit the students as it will also enhance your CV and, hopefully, give you a sense of pride. There is no simpler pleasure than talking to someone enthusiastic to listen.

And remember, always be good to people on the way up because you're going to need their help if you're ever on your way down.

STEP 3: REVIEWING YOUR GOALS

Once a year, check your goals. Are they still your goals? Have you changed what you want out of life? How far are you from getting those goals? What do you need to do in order to achieve them?

STEP 4: LEARNING ABOUT YOURSELF

Learning about yourself is probably one of the most important things you can do. The vast majority of companies that have proper management and staff development programmes use psychometric testing as their main tool. There is no reason you too can't use these powerful tools to help you grow and understand yourself.

The most famous (and perhaps most popular) psycho-metric testing system is the Myers–Briggs system. Developed by Katherine Briggs and her daughter Isobel Briggs, it works on the theories of Jung. If you want to know the background there are plenty of books/websites willing to explain them. Basically, it works on the assumption that there are sixteen distinct personality types, based on eight different personal traits. The system uses a questionnaire to find your preferences – for example, if you prefer to use sensing (i.e. using observation and facts to gather information) or whether you prefer intuition (i.e. looking for patterns, as many possibilities as possible and using speculation).

The result of the questionnaire is a four-letter code (for example, ENTP). This code only reveals your preferences for the way you think and act in certain situations. It helps you learn about your strengths. For example, an ENTP should be good at a broad range of things. He or she enjoys debating and is resourceful but prone to neglect routine and to be outspoken. Typically an ENTP is excited by new ideas.

The advantage of knowing this sort of information about yourself is that you can use it to decode the way you work – so if your natural preference is to avoid deadlines, you know your highest stress levels come when you have a deadline looming. You could, of course, use that knowledge to change careers to where your natural preferences lie, or you could use it to help you strengthen your weaknesses and to control your stress levels. For example, ENTPs enjoy deadlines but only when they're really cutting it fine. While this works most of the time, it will sometimes let them down. They might be better off setting a false deadline in order to do the work before it's needed rather than when it's actually needed.

The truth is that you can only play to your strengths when you know what your strengths really are. There are plenty of ways to go about taking these tests:

- Ask your company if they run this sort of testing (many large companies do) or if they are willing to run it.

- Look in *Yellow Pages* to find a local psychologist or career counsellor who is trained and licensed to run the test he or she is selling.

- Look on the web. There are plenty of sites offering online testing, although you miss the benefit of having a trained person to talk you through the results and how to use them.

For the truly fearless, there is a free online test at www.keirsey.com. It will give you a Myers-Briggs code, which you can then use to read up on your personality type. But remember, the most important thing is to use these tests as a tool for your own self-development. Use the knowledge of your strengths and weaknesses to help you grow.

STEP 5: GETTING READY FOR PROMOTION OR YOUR NEXT CAREER

Keep your mind open to the skills you might require later in your career progression. These might be skills you need for your promotion or skills that are fundamental to your next chosen career. Flicking through job ads and keeping note of the sort of jobs that appeal to you is a useful method.

Review what skills you might need to acquire and work out how you're going to get them. Set yourself goals. Don't forget, if you can't get the skills you need in your present job, there are always training courses, voluntary and charitable organisations and hobbies to help you get them. Then, when it's time to move up or out, you'll be ready to make a successful move.

Final Words

Congratulations! Hopefully, you're just accepted a job or are weighing up the difference between two or more fantastic offers. Or perhaps you've just read this book and are about to start your journey.

No matter what stage of your job hunt you have reached, your experiences are invaluable to us so, if we've missed something, let us know. We will respond personally either by email, or by post if you include an SAE. We can't promise to reply to everyone but we'll do our best and, perhaps, with your permission, we'll use the information in compiling the next edition.

Lastly, when you finally sign that contract, don't forget to reward yourself for all that hard work. You've earned it!

Benjamin Scott and Michael Collins
c/o How To Books
3 Newtec Place
Magdalen Road
Oxford OX4 1RE
Degreeintoacareer@howtobooks.co.uk

Appendices

A: PURSUING POSTGRADUATE STUDY

Postgraduate education is a tempting proposition, especially if you can get someone else to pay for it. You can put off decisions about your career and future and you can feel good about yourself believing that your hard work enhances your prospects. However, be warned, it can be a waste of your time and money. You need to know not only what you are taking on but, more importantly, why you are taking on a postgraduate course.

Remember, universities make big money out of postgraduate studies: just look at the fees charged. It is in their best interests to convince you that any further degree will enhance your prospects of a highflying career. They peddle a range of postgraduate study options, including:

- masters (MA, MSc, etc.);
- doctorates (PhD, etc.);
- research masters (MPhil) which lead to a PhD; and
- postgraduate certificates and diplomas.

Benefits of masters and diplomas
If you really want a return on the time and money you invest into any postgraduate qualification, it must fit into your career strategy. If you have a good reason to take a

course – i.e. it's a prerequisite for your dream career (for example, a PGCE for teaching) – take it for that reason alone. Many post-graduate diplomas are done in a different field from the first degree in order to further a career option (for example, a law-conversion diploma).

However, qualifications that are not required as a starting point within an industry (unlike a PGCE) need to be considered very carefully. No degree certificate is intrinsically worth anything. It will be down to you how you use any postgraduate study to further your career. In other words, how will you sell the benefits of your masters degree to an employer? And, as we've said before, your answer will be based on the skills and knowledge you have gained that will help their business and make you stand out from the competition.

Masters can be very good investments for the future because they:

◆ help you stand out from the pack of the ever-growing number of graduates;

◆ are relatively cheap and only take up a year, plus you can choose to do one in almost anything; and

◆ help rectify a potential damaging low first degree. It may be your first degree is poor for a range of reasons (effects of an illness, personal circumstances, playing too much sport or just laziness). However, a masters can deflect most of that damage. It'll demonstrate your determination to succeed and rise above your previous failures and, with a bit of work experience, will make your CV look solid, if not special.

Disadvantages of PhDs

Generally speaking, unless you really want to get into university, lecturing or research positions, never attempt a PhD. High-level academic research is fascinating and extremely satisfying, but it's also specialised. From an employer's point of view, while it looks impressive, it generally adds almost nothing to your previous degrees.

Even if you're after a university-based career, there are no guarantees a PhD will secure a job for you. Just look at the figures if you don't believe us. There are over two thousand history PhD students. Even assuming half either drop out or are mature students, that still leaves a thousand potential PhD graduates competing for the same number of research and higher education posts. Speak to any university selection panels and they'll tell you the numbers of applicants are growing and that starting salaries are being reduced.

PhDs, in comparison to masters, offer low returns for time and effort expended. Arguably, science-based PhDs are an asset, especially for moves into industry, but are they more of an asset than four years' working in that sector? And, if you want to end up in the school/teaching sector, you probably would have been better off with a PGCE plus an MA to help fast-track you to a headship.

The most important thing to remember about postgraduate study, especially PhDs, is the effect it will have on your financial future. Your first career, whatever you have chosen, will be delayed by four, five or six years. If you pursue an academic career you'll be delayed even longer.

A round of fellowships, short contracts and part-time work is the norm, before a permanent post is usually attained. This can all affect how you finance your old age (which we know is the last thing on your mind, but it is very important). Any delays in gaining permanent employment can even stop you qualifying for a full state pension, let alone a full university pension, or even a decent personal pension. This will matter unless you are prepared to trade off potential personal poverty against a stimulating career.

Postgraduate degrees are tools to be used by you for your *own* strategy. If a postgraduate qualification appeals to you because you don't want to work for someone else or join a rat race, why not consider other directions as well, such as setting up your own business (you can have the stimulation *and* the rewards).

Unless pursuing qualifications required for a specific career, always look at adding value to your existing degree. If your choice of subject is not set by your future career plans, do your masters/diploma in another subject (for example, adding international relations, a language or, even, computers to a history degree is ideal).

Remember, the universities aren't going anywhere. You can always come back to university when you have the money, the house and the kids have grown up. You can enjoy and indulge yourself without worrying about what you're going to do afterwards.

B: FURTHER READING AND LINKS

As we said before, there are thousands of books covering between them every aspects of job-hunting, including those focused on particular markets, such as a single country (for example, the USA) or an entire industry (for example, advertising). Every library and bookshop has a different selection of titles on display – so there is little point in listing them all here. You will find that, whichever books you read, some will contain *both* gems and nonsense, so keep that 'bullshit antenna' finely tuned. Here are a handful of titles that might be useful:

- *Po: Beyond Yes and No* by Edward de Bono (International Centre for Creative Thinking, 1990). Or any of his other books on lateral thinking – an ideal introduction to thinking in a different direction.

- *Writing that Works* by Kenneth Roman and Joel Raphaelson (HarperResource, 2000). A concise and effective writing guide – pithy and well priced.

- *How to Win Friends and Influence People* by Dale Carnegie (Simon & Schuster, 1981). The original book about how to impress people by a master salesman.

- *People Types and Tiger Stripes* by G. Laurence (Center for the Application of Psychological Type, Grainesville, FL). A useful guide to personality typing.

Trade magazines

If you can't find a trade magazine for the industry you're after, try looking for one using the following:

- *The Writer's Handbook* or *The Writers' and Artists' Yearbook.*

- http://directory.google.com/Top/Business/Resources/News_and_Publications/Magazines/Trade

- www.britishservices.co.uk

Internet search engines

The following search engines might be useful:

- www.dogpile.com
- www.google.co.uk

Job sites

Try the following:

- www.jobserve.com
- www.monster.co.uk
- www.totaljobs.com
- www.fish4jobs.com
- www.gojobsite.co.uk
- www.planetrecruit.co.uk
- www.workthing.co.uk
- www.jobs.guardian.co.uk
- www.jobsearch.co.uk
- www.prospects.ac.uk

Taking a break from job-hunting – and reading something for fun

You might find the following useful relief from job-hunting:

- *Vurt* by Jeff Noon (Fourth Estate, 1993).

- *Canal Dreams* by Iain Banks (Little, Brown & Co., 2001).

- *Northern Lights* by Philip Pullman (Scholastic, 1995).

- *The Wind Singer* by William Nicholson (Egmont, 2002).

- *Cat's Cradle* by Kurt Vonnegut (Penguin Books, 1999).

C: TIPS FOR THE WORLD OF WORK

The first day

Make sure you know where you're going. If you've got a letter from your new employer, then, great. If not, give whoever is going to be your boss a ring and ask him or her what time he or she would like you to start on your first day, and perhaps what the dress code is. Try to dress slightly smarter than the dress code to make a good first impression – after all, now you've got the job you need to prove you can do it. And keep all the stuff from your interview survival kit with you, just in case you get a headache or an attack of nerves.

Don't be afraid to ask questions or to make a note of what people are telling you. And don't worry about remembering names – no one gets everyone's names on the first day – just try to remember as many as you can.

The pitfalls and nightmares of being a graduate

Sometimes being the 'graduate' means being the glorified

photocopier, or even a punch-bag. Apart from just being the new kid in town (difficult on any steps of the career ladder), you might also be seen as separate from other staff. You might be seen as 'special' or 'above other people', especially on fast-track management schemes. Aside from the basic prejudice, the main reason for this is that you have everything to prove – you need to show everyone you are a real employee not just the graduate. As long as you work hard and demonstrate your value, these walls will soon tumble.

Be aware that some graduates suffer from a 'culture shock' in their first real job – working life is very different from university life. Just remember, you will adapt. Within a few months it will all seem like the normal way of doing things.

Personality clashes do happen. Most companies take a responsible attitude and will be willing to discuss the issues and help to resolve them. If you've just started the job, give it a few months to see if you're just reacting badly. Remember, you can always leave. There are plenty of opportunities out there – not only with different companies in the same industry but also in different industries and careers. The choice is yours, and you can always choose again.

The following is a list of some pearls of wisdom that might help you to succeed in your new job.

Some 'gems' for success

✓ Manage other people's expectation of your work – don't allow other people to pressurise you into failing to meet their targets. Give yourself a margin of error – it's always better to do something earlier or below budget.

✓ Be aware that while there is only one company (or organisation), there are many employees. These individuals make up the political structure of the company – they hold the power. So take time to understand everyone and how they influence others.

✓ Be ready to absorb other people's envy and to be invisible on occasions. It's not always the wisest thing to be seen all the time – only at the right moments.

✓ Treat everyone as a customer – from the people you work with to the real customers. It doesn't matter if they like you or not as long as they are satisfied with your work.

✓ Become used to, and live off, change. Need we say more? It's not easy but it will benefit you. As soon as change starts happening, don't resist it, see if you can benefit from it.

✓ Always speed up – the more you work, the better you should be at the basics. They should, in theory, start taking less and less time so you can concentrate on the more important issues.

✓ Accept ambiguity and uncertainty – otherwise your career will become very stressful. The future is unpredictable – get used to it.

✓ Keep a score of your successes to help demonstrate your value during any appraisals or evaluation meetings.

✓ See yourself as a service centre/company: if you don't know something, offer to find out (and do it so you know next time). If you go that extra mile for everyone, it'll really impresses them (i.e. don't just say 'the number will be in *Yellow Pages*', offer to look it up and tell them the number.

✓ Don't think about your tasks as being 'jobs to do': think of the people you're doing them for instead – 'the customers you're helping'.

✓ Keep up your self-branding – develop it and change it slowly. Once you allow your reputation to sour it'll take a long time to rebuild it. Think about your image and how others perceive you.

✓ Practise self-improvement – take joy in learning new things and better ways of doing old things. If your company doesn't believe in training (fools, if they don't), give yourself training. Follow areas that interest you. The more skills you have, the easier it'll be to change careers or companies.

✓ And, finally, manage your motivation and take care of yourself both spiritually and mentally. There's no point allowing work to crush you – you're worth more than that!

D: ANSWERS TO THE APTITUDE TESTS

Practice test 1
Verbal questions: 1. c; 2. d; 3. a; 4. d

Numerical questions: 1. d; 2. c; 3. d
Numerical analysis questions: 1. c; 2. e; 3. b; 4. a.

Practice test 2
Passage 1 questions: 1. a; 2. b; 3. a
Passage 2 questions: 1. b; 2. a; 3. c
Numerical questions: 1. b; 2. d; 3. b; 4. d; 5. b; 6. c

Guide to Questions and Answers

Index